HOW TO ORGANIZE YOUR WORK AND YOUR LIFE

REVISED

ROBERT MOSKOWITZ

HOW TO ORGANIZE YOUR WORK AND YOUR LIFE

REVISED

MAIN STREET BOOKS

DOUBLEDAY

NEW YORK   LONDON   TORONTO   SYDNEY   AUCKLAND

A MAIN STREET BOOK
PUBLISHED BY DOUBLEDAY
a division of Bantam Doubleday Dell Publishing Group, Inc.
1540 Broadway, New York, New York 10036

MAIN STREET BOOKS, DOUBLEDAY, and the portrayal of a building
with a tree are trademarks of Doubleday,
a division of Bantam Doubleday Dell Publishing Group, Inc.

BOOK DESIGN BY GLEN M. EDELSTEIN

Library of Congress Cataloging-in-Publication Data

Moskowitz, Robert.
    How to organize your work and your life / by Robert Moskowitz. —
2nd rev. ed.
        p.   cm.
    Includes index.
    1. Executives—Time management.   2. Businessmen—Time management.
I. Title.
HD38.2.M675   1993
658.4′093—dc20   92-27756
                                                                          CIP

ISBN 0-385-42480-9
Copyright © 1981, 1993 by Robert Moskowitz

1 2 3 4 5 6 7 8 9 10

Second Edition

This book is dedicated to my lovely wife, Francine, without whose support and great insight into human personality I would never have discovered what I know about productivity and effectiveness, and certainly would never have completed this book; and to my sons, Jake and Alex, of whom I am very proud, and who continually prove convincingly to me that no matter how productive or effective one may be, no one is a hero in one's own home.

CONTENTS

CHAPTER 7: Married (or Unmarried) with Children 186

Organizing Your Child-Rearing Time 187
Organizing Your Child-Rearing Equipment 188
Organizing Your Child-Rearing Travel 190
Organizing Your Children's Caregivers 194
Organizing Your Child-Rearing Finances 196
When Parents Live Apart 197

CHAPTER 8: A Concise Program for the Busy Business
Executive 201

Measure Your Present Results 202
How to Establish Your Priorities 203
How to Begin Planning Your Days and Weeks 204
Ten Great Effectiveness Builders You Can Use Immediately 206
Estimation Procedure for the Business Executive 216

CHAPTER 9: A Concise Program for the Busy Lawyer,
Accountant, or Other Professional 218

Keep Track of Your Billable Time 219
How to Establish Your Priorities 221
Allocate Your Efforts 222
Learn to Work in Concentrated Bursts 223
Ten Great Effectiveness Builders You Can Use Immediately 226
Estimation Procedure for the Professional 232

CHAPTER 10: A Concise Program for the Busy "At Home"
Person 234

Define Who Does What and When They Do It 235
Identify Your Current Patterns 236
Define What You Will and Won't Do 236
Make a Schedule You Can Live With 240
How to Get Your Life Under Control 242
Be Ruthless About What You Have Time For 245
A Place (and Time) for Everything 247
Three Ways to Faster Shopping 248
Estimation Procedure for the Busy "At Home" Person 249

INTRODUCTION TO THE REVISED EDITION

Since first published in 1981, *How to Organize Your Work and Your Life* has been very well received year after year. But life in modern America has a way of changing rapidly, and a book originally written at the beginning of the 1980s to help people get the most from life can now benefit a great deal from expansion and revision to meet the changing demands and lifestyles of Americans as we rush toward the end of the century.

In a real sense, America is only now catching up with the material in this book. One of the fastest-growing employment trends in the '90s is the accelerating acceptance of telework, or telecommuting—the practice of working one or more days at home or at a local office (often shared) in order to reduce the number of long trips to the one's regular (often centralized) office. Experience shows that the efficiencies of telecommuting—reduced pollution, less time wasted in the car or on the train, lower energy costs, reduced stress, and so forth—are obtained only when managers and telecommuters have their work (and their lives) organized well enough to remain effective outside the traditional office environment. Telecommuters will find the information in this book invaluable for increasing productivity both inside and outside the traditional office setting.

A major change in American life has been the growing number of separated partners—as well as traditional families—with young children. Virtually everyone raising children is under a great deal of pressure from all aspects of their life and work, and feels crushed between conflicting responsibilities, opportunities, and objectives. To help make sense of child rearing in today's more complex world, I've added all-new material on dealing with the time demands and organizational problems involved. These are priceless skills for parents who feel hard-pressed to give their children "quality time" without sacrificing their careers or their romantic and personal time together. Men and women who have separated or divorced face different—but equally important and oppressive—time demands and organizational problems surrounding the fair and emotionally healthy sharing of child-rearing responsibilities. Anyone with children should benefit from this discussion and its practical suggestions.

Two other important aspects of life as we lead it today are: a) developing and maintaining a second income, and b) going back to school for additional credentials. The second income is often earned from something like teaching a course in the evenings or running a sideline business, but it can result from any productive activity that catches your interest and has a market value. Budding entrepreneurs and stuggling wage earners will now find in this edition a solid portfolio of useful suggestions and strategies for organizing their extra efforts. Similarly, many people are going back to school for advanced degrees. Trying to walk a line somewhere between the free-form time of the student and the tight scheduling of the full-time employee or professional creates a demanding lifestyle that requires the specialized information I've added to this edition of *How to Organize Your Work and Your Life*.

In my continuing pursuit of efficiency and organization and in the investigations into the fruitful use of time and personal energy I have done since first finishing this book, I have discovered two new areas that demand inclusion in this revised version: the power of the creative use of procrastination, and the relationships between time, organization, effectiveness, and money.

Many think that proscrastination is always a time-management problem or an organizational dodge. I have discovered that this is far from the truth. Procrastination can be a favorable weapon in the fight to get and stay organized. To this end, I have identified and developed a few critically important principles and tactics that can help you determine when to use procrastination profitably and when to avoid it. The trick is not only to know the proper techniques but to recognize when to apply them.

The first thought about getting organized and improving effectiveness often centers around devoting more time to certain tasks. In certain situations, however, people can organize better and achieve more satisfactory results through a different approach— that of spending a specific combination of time and money rather than time only. As with procrastination, most people have powerful preconceptions about money's role in helping them become more organized and happier. Yet I have learned, and can show, that virtually everyone has the little bit of money required to improve dramatically the organization of his or her work and life.

One of the most prominent changes to occur since I first wrote *How to Organize Your Work and Your Life* has been the proliferation of personal computers throughout our homes and businesses. These machines have transformed my own life and have proved invaluable in helping me organize my thoughts, my resources, and my professional activities. Practically everyone I know has been buffeted by the computer revolution on the job, and millions of Americans have brought a computer into their homes. Although we face even more dramatic changes in the years to come, I have liberally laced this revision with many practical suggestions and strategies for using personal computers to great advantage in organizing your life and your work.

Clearly, the world has changed a great deal since I first completed *How to Organize Your Work and Your Life*. Now that I've rewritten the material to take into account the most recent understandings of lifestyle and effectiveness, and have included all-new material on computers, second incomes, and people choosing to work at home, along with techniques for mastering procrastination and for coping with the demands of child rearing, the book is totally revamped— and fully equipped to provide as much (or more) support for people during the coming decade as it has during the previous one.

HOW TO ORGANIZE YOUR WORK AND YOUR LIFE

REVISED

CHAPTER 1

THE BASICS OF GETTING RESULTS

How much time do you have left? How many more goals and achievements do you want to attain?

When you strip away all the camouflage and get right to the heart of the matter, you're a serious, capable person who has more than enough ambition. You take your commitments and responsibilities to heart. In your own way, you honestly try your best to achieve what you want, what you promise, and what is expected of you.

But the time goes so fast! And sometimes it seems as though Murphy's Law—"Anything that can go wrong will go wrong"—is the dominant law of the universe. Even when your private life and your job are going smoothly, you find it takes too long to reach your goals, to attain what you want. And as you progress, you generally want to do, see, and accomplish even more.

This book can change all that for you. It gives you a method of organizing everything you do, everything you want to do, and everything you must and must not do. It gives you a system of principles, ideas, and specific actions to speed up every project and every effort, and help you get what you want much quicker, easier, sooner.

What holds you back right now is the tremendous amount of wasted time, misdirected energy, and subtle "friction" in so much of what you do. Whether you admit it or not, a good portion of every day goes down the drain, and you use too much of what's left without thinking, without direction, without a Master Plan. With this book to guide you, though, and with the personal notebook it enables you to put together out of your own experiences, you can change all that. You will accomplish more every hour, every day of your life. You will understand the *philosophical,* the *managerial,* and the *technical* aspects of effectiveness, and learn to see dozens of better ways to direct and control your efforts to push yourself toward the rewards you want and to hold back from trivial or worthless pursuits.

These are the benefits you'll find in this book. And they extend to anyone who embraces its principles, actions, and ideas. Whether you are a tan-worshipping lawyer in the Sun Belt or a radio producer in Cincinnati, an aspiring painter in New York or a parent home in Atlanta all day with demanding children, the material in this book can open a new world of satisfaction and achievement, no matter what your goals may be.

But general talk like this will not improve your effectiveness or change your method of handling opportunities. You need motivation to make changes. And nothing is more motivating than a specific look at the details of what you can hope to gain. Here's a chance to give yourself that look right now.

Experience 1

Self-Evaluation: Benefits You Can Expect from Boosting Your Effectiveness

Instructions: Start a personal notebook using any 5-by-8 or 8½-by-11-inch permanent or loose-leaf binder. On a clean page, list eight of the most important projects and activities in your life and/or your career that you feel you have been neglecting recently. For this Experience, don't ask for help: stick with your own evaluations, judgments, and standards of importance. If you feel you are neglecting your professional education or your physical fitness, for example, you'll feel better after working to improve this. If you listen to other people, they may not recognize this particular problem, or they may convince you there are more important ones.

Once you have identified your neglected projects and activities, list for each one the benefits you expect when you complete the project or undertake the activity.

Experience 1 is valuable because it helps you specify some of the most immediate and concrete results you can obtain. Once you identify some neglected projects and activities, you can focus your thinking on them as you go through the ideas, principles, and techniques in the rest of this book. Test your new knowledge and your new organization/effectiveness skills on these activities whenever you can. The more directly you tie the material in this book to such important activities, the more you will benefit.

The results of Experience 1 help you focus on the rewards you will gain as a result of being more effective. You can have them if you change your habits and procedures. If you don't believe you can obtain satisfying and desirable benefits from better methods, if you don't try these ideas and techniques in your own situation, you are doing yourself a terrible disservice.

The most frequent reason for carrying on with less effective procedures is uncertainty. You may feel uncertain about the value of these methods. You may feel you can't change, or that any changes you do make won't be worthwhile. You are wrong.

Achievement, success, and high levels of effectiveness are not determined by your genes. You learn how to get what you want from the world around you, and sometimes you learn how not to. Without knowing it, you set your own achievement level according to the example of the people and situations around you. It's a haphazard process, at best, not always fully accomplished, and the problems in learning how to succeed often stop a person well short of his or her highest potential. If you are not happy with the results you are presently getting in your life, you're in luck. You are now holding the very instrument to help you change, improve, and attain more of what you want! You can have what you want starting now. All you must do is read. I will do the rest.

KNOW WHERE YOU ARE HEADED

Visualize yourself in the Caribbean. It's warm. It's sunny. There's no particular danger: We've banished all sharks and jellyfish. But you have the natural urge to get back on dry land. Yet, alone and adrift, you don't know either where you are or which direction to go. Now imagine you spot an island. Suddenly, you have a direction! Your pulse quickens, you feel a burst of motivation. You look for a way to reach the island, then exert yourself and make it! Your sighting of a goal brought everything else into focus, including the wind, the tide, the current, your own strength and fitness. While a great many factors helped determine whether or not you reached the island, the process began only *after* you sighted a goal.

What if you had never looked around you? What if you had merely been drifting, preoccupied only with your immediate surroundings? You might have passed, unknowingly, within two hundred yards of a bountiful island paradise. And if no rescuer had come out to get you, you would never even have seen the paradise as you drifted past! The point is this: You must not only be concerned with your immediate surroundings, you must constantly scan the horizon for new and better opportunities for achievement.

So take a look around in your present life and work. Do you know what accomplishments would make today satisfying for you? If you do, then in the most important sense you know where you are heading. You may or may not realize those accomplishments, which means you may or may not gain the satisfaction you want from your efforts. But at least you are in a position to try. Other people (and you, perhaps, on other days) have no idea what accomplishments would make the day satisfying. This means they have no basis for choosing what to do first. And if they also have no structure to give them direction, their accomplishments and feelings of satisfaction will be determined by chance or by other factors beyond their personal control.

Many people have the mistaken idea that mastering time and shaping results to suit their desires are fanciful notions, not rooted in reality. If they happen to believe in magic, they may think these techniques are a cure-all for every problem. If they don't believe in magic, they may think the skills are at best a foolish fancy, at worst a charlatan's hustle. But all these people ignore the basic practicality and realism that lie behind conscious efforts to be more effective. There is nothing fanciful about them. You start by establishing goals and achievements that will satisfy you. Nobody else, only you! No one dictates any particular goals to you, nor does anyone tell you how much effort to put in. The procedure works for everyone because it is so basic: First, determine what in the world will satisfy you, and only then concern yourself with making specific progress in those directions.

The method is so powerful that people who practice the ideas and techniques you are about to learn are a long step ahead of those who do not. Regardless of any other factors, people who organize their work and their life know where they are headed. And like the ocean drifter, they are therefore in much better condition to make whatever progress they can toward the satisfying goals they have in sight.

And you are not limited to one goal at a time, either. You can use the satisfaction of one accomplishment to fuel a separate effort toward another. You can have, and work toward, as many goals as you like. The next goal may lie two hundred miles to the west, or it may be attainable right on your island. No matter. The methods and techniques work just as well whatever it is you want to accomplish.

However, while I am not concerned with your particular goals, *you* most certainly must be. In fact, the specifics of the goals you set for yourself determine in great measure your accomplishments and, ultimately, your happiness. You need a *philosophical* understanding of what you want to achieve as you go through this book or you'll miss the chance to put what you learn into practice immediately. In essence, I must help you make your life and career goals more explicit. You will work on this throughout the book. But get started right now with Experience 2. Go through it and answer the questions as well as you can for now. Even if you cannot give a final answer to each question, be thinking about your answers as you read the rest of this book.

Experience 2

Self-Evaluation: Your Life and Career Goals

Instructions: This is a self-evaluation Experience. Only your own feelings, beliefs, ideas, and judgments are relevant to how you will work through it.

1)   In your personal notebook, make a list of ten "goals" you

would like to achieve in your *personal life* during the next ten years. Each goal should describe an achievement—or an honor or reward recognizing an achievement—you would be proud to accomplish. Try to express each goal in specifics so you or anyone else can determine whether or not you achieve it. Examples: a) establish five close friendships with people you don't already know, b) travel around the world, c) go camping in Brazil, d) learn to play five songs on the guitar. List the present activities you might have to give up to have a chance to reach each of your personal goals.

2)   In your personal notebook, make a list of ten "goals" you would like to achieve in your *career* during the next ten years. Each goal should describe an achievement—or an honor or reward recognizing an achievement—you would be proud to accomplish. Each goal should be expressed in specifics so you or anyone else can determine whether or not you achieve it. Examples: a) win an Academy Award, b) earn a promotion or a salary increase to a specific level, c) accomplish a specific project or specific amount of work by a certain deadline. List the present activities you might have to give up to have a chance to reach each of your career goals.

3)   In your personal notebook, list two other activities, accomplishments, rewards, or recognitions that would bring you the highest level of satisfaction. List the present activities you might have to give up to have a chance to make these ideas a reality.

4)   For each item you have listed, describe what further preparation you might undertake to help you along the way.

THERE'S ONLY SO MUCH TIME

Unfortunately, in a given day you just do not have enough time to take all the significant actions you dream of, the kind you anticipate for several days ahead. These might include: attending crucial meetings, visiting close friends or lovers, making life-changing or career-changing choices, watching historic sporting events, reading or writing vital reports, or other memorable experiences. Theoretically, you can make dozens of giant decisions in a single day: whether or not to purchase Arco Oil Company, fly to the moon, embark on an around-the-world cruise, or marry the person of your dreams. You can make such decisions because a decision takes only two seconds. But practically speaking, a significant action represents much more time, thought, and effort than the few seconds you need for the decision that sets it in motion. Even with single-minded determination, there's so much preparation, work, and coordination with others involved that you can rarely complete more than one or two significant actions a day. What's more, a decision is not much good unless you can take specific actions to implement it. And implementation is where your time and effort can get lost—or can result in the achievements you want.

Experience 3 is a good way to visualize the difficulty of operating without strict control. It gives you a structured method for comparing your stated goals with the de facto goals you actually work to achieve. You will probably find major discrepancies between what you want to achieve and what you actually strive to achieve. In the course of this book, you will learn to erase most or all of these discrepancies.

Experience 3

Self-Evaluation: Comparing Priorities and Activities

Instructions: This Experience helps you compare the projects and activities to which you *say* you give a high priority with the projects and activities to which you *actually* give your time.

1) In your personal notebook, list the ten projects, activities, or goals you feel are your "highest priorities" for today and/or the next few weeks. If you like, use some of the same goals you listed in Experience 2.
2) In your personal notebook, list the ten most demanding and/or most time-consuming projects, activities, or goals to which you gave time today.
3) Compare your two lists: How many of your important long-term goals or your more immediate objectives re-

ceived no attention from you today? On the other hand, how many "no priority" items—goals or objectives that never made it onto your "top ten" list—received a good portion of your effort?

Obviously, you can't work toward every goal every day. Your time and energy are limited. But these limits don't prevent you from organizing, controlling, and aiming your efforts. In fact, a minute's clear thought will show you the necessity of doing this, of making your limited opportunities count the most and yield as much as possible of what you want. To drive home this necessity, you may want to ponder the full range of your virtually insatiable desires. Experience 4 is a tool to help you.

Experience 4

Complete List of Desirable Goals

Instructions: This is a self-evaluation experience. Only your own feelings, beliefs, ideas, and judgments are relevant to how you will work it through.

1) In your personal notebook, list all the things you would like to do during your lifetime.

Samples:

PEOPLE TO SEE	PLACES TO GO	THINGS TO DO
Paul McCartney	Paris	Play in an All-Star Game
Francis Ford Coppola	The moon	Star in a film
Stash Karczewski	Suriname	Earn $1,000,000

2) Count them. How many lifetimes would you need to do them all?

When you compare your desires with your realistic potential for accomplishment, the picture becomes painfully clear: There's no way you can accomplish all your most important goals, especially when pestered by the little details of the business of living. The only way to cope with this overload—the only hope—is to focus on key goals and strive toward them.

KNOW WHAT TO SPEND TIME ON NEXT

Mastering your time has a second benefit, equally as powerful as establishing goals and equally rooted in practicality and realism. Merely having goals puts you ahead of those who have none. Once ahead, you get the second benefit: the opportunity to direct your efforts toward your goals. This gives you more results for every "unit" of effort you put in. In effect, once you know what accomplishments would satisfy you, you can more easily see—and take the proper steps to help you achieve—what you want.

In practice, this comes down to repeatedly asking yourself "What should I do next?" I refer to this as your Basic Choice, and in Chapter 3 you will learn how to ask and answer this question as second nature. Ideally, this Basic Question leads you to the one opportunity for action that gives you the best chance for the most satisfaction. Once you get the hang of setting up and making your Basic Choices, you can apply the idea very quickly in any situation. The choice you make sets a definite direction to investigate and a definite goal to pursue.

LEARN TO DO THE MOST IN THE LEAST TIME

In this book, time-saving techniques are only one part—although a vital part—of the entire organizing and achieving process.

Once you establish goals and choose your next step, you enter the arena of real-time/real-life *action*. Here is where you put theory and principle into practice. Here is where you convert all your plans, hopes, and dreams into put-up-or-shut-up performance. And here, if your actions are not fast, smooth, and directly to the point, you are in very, very big trouble.

All of us must enter this arena on a regular basis. And the results of how well we do here impact heavily on our lives. For example, driving a car on a heavily congested street or highway puts you smack in the middle of this arena. If you negotiate the traffic and reach your destination without an accident, you've been successful. If you crash, you'll pay for your mistake in time, inconvenience, and cash. No amount of talk or action can ever undo your results in the arena of real-time/real-life action.

The ability to perform superbly in this arena is one central benefit you will obtain from this book. The general skills and specific techniques you learn here will work in an assortment of situations. And not only will you get the job done quickly, smoothly, and directly, you will save time.

Knowing how to perform well in the real-time/real-life arena has three related parts to it: a) knowing the principles behind controlled accomplishment; b) knowing appropriate techniques for working faster, better, and smoother; and c) knowing yourself and your personal patterns. You can get the first two right out of this book. But to learn the third, you must look in a mirror.

The best sort of mirror to show you how you operate would be a real-time, twenty-four-hour-a-day videotape, with the camera following you everywhere. Since the chances of your arranging for that service are practically nil, count on getting the same knowledge of yourself a bit differently.

The primary tool for learning about your personal patterns and what they reveal about you is the Time Log. Something like counting calories to lose weight, this is a detailed record you keep over a period of several weeks. Here's how it works: Every few minutes, you record (in one second or less) how you have spent the time since you last marked your Log. At the end of each day, you have used only a minute or two to make a complete record of where you put all your time. At the end of several weeks, you have a complete record that reveals: a) details of how you spend your time, b) your overall patterns of behavior, c) opportunities for concentrating on your more important goals, d) possibilities for holding back from unimportant projects or activities, and e) habits you can learn that automatically make you more effective. You can find directions for using a very effective Time Log method in Appendix A.

KNOW WHEN TO WORK ON EACH ITEM

One young woman I know has a career, a family, and an itch to go back to school. Between all three, she has dozens of "important" projects and activities all clamoring for her interest and attention. Before she can even finish one item, several more are insisting on immediate attention. In fact, she is so "busy" she cannot allow herself to become fully immersed even in her favorite projects. If she did, she might pay "too much" attention to one and have to shortchange another. Her days are madhouse encounters, a constant stream of commitments and activities all requiring action—like trying to fit twenty-five square pegs into fifteen round holes. She pays absolutely no attention to her Basic Choice because she feels herself to be at the mercy of her tasks. At every hesitation, two or three items invariably rear their heads and demand attention.

This brings us into the realm of *managing* your goals—the fine art of packing every day with just enough of the most useful activities. Too tight, and you'll lose time and energy to unavoidable distractions, interruptions, and emergencies. Too loose, and you'll simply waste your skills and abilities. The idea is to have every day—and every project—under your own executive control, and thus be able to make the best choices regarding when to work on each and every item.

Most people find it hard to recognize the right time to turn to a particular project or activity. As a result, most people don't bother managing their own activities. They simply work on whatever catches their interest, until either: a) something else catches their interest, or b) something or someone else grabs them and pushes them, face-first, into a new project or activity.

A pattern like this makes it hard for anyone to achieve what he or she wants. When outside factors have too much control over your days, your own desires go out the window. Until you take back control of your efforts and your energy, your effectiveness will suffer—and so will your hopes and dreams.

To take that control, you need to know and act on the following information:

a) The relative importance of each item facing you
b) The amount of time each item will require from you for optimum results

c) The amount of time between the present moment and
   the deadline for each item
d) Your current capacities, strengths, and weaknesses

This may seem like a great deal of unrelated information. But it goes right to the main point of choosing what to do next, and you can keep track of it all quite easily. In fact, that's the simplest part, as you'll learn in later sections of this book. With practice and experience, you will be sniffing out this information as easily as you now see the color of every item of paperwork facing you.

Most people find it much harder to *act* on the basis of this information: to pick and choose, from all the items you could work on, the *one* item that takes you most directly toward your desired objectives right now.

KNOW THE PEOPLE TO TURN TO

Achieving what you want doesn't happen in a vacuum. As much as 90 percent of your effectiveness comes from people—people like you and me who take action to create results, or who use human resources skillfully to accomplish their desired purposes.

Very few of us can accomplish our goals individually. Most jobs, most private lives, and most personal dreams are intimately caught up with the work, the lives, and the personalities of people around us. In a real sense, everything comes down to its impact on people. You can ignore the people factor if you wish. You can mechanically try to achieve what you want by forcing through changes and treating people like units. But you can get much better results if you use all your skill and talent to work with people as smoothly as you work with forms, figures, and equipment. And if you must emphasize one side of your skills more than another, your people-oriented skills will probably prove more useful.

Sometimes, you can achieve more of what you want simply by taking advantage of your personal contacts and affiliations. This is probably nothing new to you. People have been turning to friends, relatives, and acquaintances since cavemen first cooperated in a dinosaur hunt. Experience 5 gives you a start toward organizing and keeping track of the people you know. The idea is to use this list of your human resources as a tool in your effort to accomplish your purposes. Whatever you want to accomplish, whatever help you need, you can look at Your Human Resources Checklist to see if you know someone to whom you can turn. As you expand your contacts, you will soon find you can obtain much of the help you want and need from the people on your list.

Experience 5

Your Human Resources Checklist

Instructions: In your personal notebook, create a series of Checklists with information on each of the people you might conceivably ask for information or advice. Keep all the Checklists handy and update them when you make new contacts or learn new information about people you already know. Then, whenever you feel the need for help, advice, or special treatment, go over your Checklists to see if you know anyone who can help you.

Here's a sample entry to show what each listing should contain (at a minimum):

Person's name	John Fluff
Phone numbers (home) (work)	212-555-5555 / 212-666-6666
Company name	Two Penguin Ice Cream Company
Job title	President
Special knowledge	Ice cream flavors; financing; good at setting up a sales force; knows what people will buy
Special skills	Very persuasive; good at backgammon
Special access	Has library card at the university
Special contacts	Knows the president of the Rotary

If you take the time to enter this information in a personal computer database, or even a word processing program, you can more easily shuffle through the people you know and find the ones who can help you with any particular project or goal.

People are often the most effective information sources. You can find the answers to questions, get advice and ideas from people three to five times faster than you can get comparable information. For example, a research assistant once spent dozens of hours poring over science texts in a fruitless effort to understand some complex details of gravity, light waves, and other aspects of electromagnetic radiation. Finally, he gave up on textbooks and began looking for someone to help him. He quickly located an expert in his own town, and in just one four-hour interview he learned the answers to all of his original questions, plus a few extras that occurred to him as he listened and understood.

In many situations, the simple act of coordinating the actions of a group of people can instantly accelerate their effectiveness (and yours) by 20 to 50 percent. For example, a group of citizens hoping to get a referendum on the local city ballot were each spending about ten hours a week planning their efforts and collecting signatures on the necessary petition. Once they began coordinating their efforts, however, they successfully gathered the needed signatures in just six hours a week per person.

WHAT YOU CAN DO

In this book, you can learn a whole new way to operate in the world, a method that is careful, thoughtful, and, above all, effective. Someday, techniques for achieving what you want will be taught in public schools. They will be recognized as a basic part of the modern curriculum, as basic as driver or sex education. While the idea of teaching these techniques may seem bizarre, after you have been through this book, you will agree that the skills you have begun to develop are:

• Results-oriented
• Useful in almost any situation

- Practical and easy to apply
- Flexible enough to suit anyone
- An effectiveness-booster that really works

For these reasons, the study of effective organization and achievement techniques is for everyone who has something he or she would seriously like to accomplish.

CHAPTER 2

YOUR LIFE AND CAREER GOALS WILL SET YOUR DIRECTION

Goals are the first step in any serious effort to improve your effectiveness and accomplish what you want in your work and your life. First of all, you need them just to measure your progress. Until you have a goal or a set of goals in front of you, there is no way to measure whether you are achieving any more or less—or getting any better or worse results—than you were before.

Even more important, goals are the basic directional arrows of your life. To illustrate this, consider the underground Métro in Paris. Whenever you travel on this system, you choose your direction by heading toward a *Destination:* the last station on the particular line. This may be Porte de la Villette, for example, or Porte d'Orléans. If you want to go in a different direction, you simply follow the signs to a different *Destination,* such as Porte Dauphine or Charenton-Écoles. During your journey, you may transfer from one train line to another, from one direction to another, many times. Most of the time, you leave a train before its last stop. But you always keep track of where you are headed by noting the ultimate destination of the train you are riding.

Goals serve the same function in your work and your life. (They serve other functions as well, but let's concentrate on this one for now.) You don't have to arrive at your goal for it to have provided a worthwhile direction. In fact, most goals are not reached. As in the Paris Métro, most times we don't travel all the way to the end of the line. Most times we simply exchange one goal for another and keep moving.

And there's nothing wrong with exchanging goals quite often. In general, you should feel perfectly free to adopt a goal for as long as it suits you, then exchange it for some other objective when the time seems right.

Face it: There's little or no virtue in sticking to a goal that no longer feels right to you. A century ago, for example, it was fashionable to think that from his youth on, a serious gentleman should totally dedicate himself to a lifetime goal, often a financial one. People who did not persevere in one major effort in this way were said to be frivolous.

Changing your goals is one good way—a perfectly fair way—to be sure you accomplish what you want. The paradox is this: You can achieve more of what you want if you quickly abandon your unreasonable goals. You see, with the same time and effort you might expend struggling toward—but not reaching—one unreasonably difficult goal, you can reach and accomplish several smaller but still desirable ones. Goals you cannot achieve with a reasonable effort are not rewarding, and they are not motivating, either. Instead, they sap your strength and make you more likely to settle for limited success on other, easier goals, when you shouldn't. When attainment of a goal is too much to hope for with reasonable effort, you can usually make more progress in a different direction.

The best goals lie in a middle ground between dearly sought-after goals that may be impossible to achieve and meaningless goals you can reach without effort. All of us need some sort of goals to provide direction to our lives and our efforts. Now the problem becomes: what kind of goals, how difficult, how long-range, how flexible?

TYPES OF GOALS

Goals break down into two basic categories: externally imposed and self-imposed. Each category has a representative motivational profile: a pattern of rewards, threats, and sources of satisfaction that helps determine how, when, and even whether you will exert yourself to achieve the goal. It's useful to recognize the various categories and types of goals so you can better control your responses to each one.

Externally Imposed Goals

My father used to suffer from too many externally imposed goals. For example, he had to learn to dance when he and my mother planned an ocean cruise. He didn't care much for dancing, and he didn't set this goal for himself. But nevertheless he had to meet it.

Externally imposed goals tend to be inflexible, often absolute, dictated by outside forces that leave little or no room for compromise or negotiation. And the strongest external forces seem to impose the most obnoxious, demanding goals. Externally imposed goals can be further categorized into personally, impersonally, and organizationally imposed goals, according to the source of the imposition. For example, a child who couldn't care less has the goal of making the school orchestra imposed by eager parents. This is an externally imposed goal of the personal type. When you are driven to look for shelter by a sudden rain squall, you are responding to an externally imposed goal; impersonal type. An executive who dislikes detail work is given the assignment of sifting stacks of financial records to find a few financial ratios or a history of past performance. This is an externally imposed goal; organizational type.

We never accept externally imposed goals freely, but are forced to accept them—in most cases as the lesser evil of a choice we never wanted.

Externally imposed goals of the organizational type include all the job assignments, performance specifications, and behavioral demands employers make on employees. A classic example: the employer who asks his management people to accomplish 10 percent more this year than last with the same budget and resource allocations. Or consider the organization that changes its data processing procedures. Suddenly, everyone concerned with timely information must learn to work with new routines, regulations, and demands.

There is nothing intrinsically wrong with a goal imposed on you by your organization. While it may or may not be interesting, challenging, or exciting, it may offer you some personal satisfaction. But most often, the organization benefits more from your accomplishments than you do.

This is too bad. In many situations, the people who set up the organizational goals could and should set goals that, when achieved, would benefit both workers and the organization. This adjustment would tune the motivational profile of the organizationally imposed goal to fit the people asked to accomplish it. The impact would be to produce much higher levels of motivation, achievement, and success.

In the absence of such goal direction on your job, you must take your own steps to make your work-related goals more satisfying and rewarding. The techniques you will learn as you go through this book will enable you to "hang" many goals on your special motivational "hooks." The effect is to supercharge your motivation level and make you more eager and more likely to reach these goals.

Self-Imposed Goals

You almost always get some direct satisfaction from every self-imposed goal you achieve. If you didn't, you probably wouldn't set the goal.

Self-imposed goals are the ones we hear about in storybooks or made-for-TV movies. For example, the story of the poor boy who becomes a millionaire is a story of a self-imposed goal. The athlete who overcomes incredible obstacles to win the gold medal is also responding to a self-imposed goal. Achievements aimed at self-imposed goals often extract your finest efforts and bring you tremendous feelings of satisfaction and self-worth along with whatever tangible rewards they may earn.

Once you think about it, you probably won't feel surprised to realize your self-imposed goal are usually the most motivating. They start out linked to huge pools of emotional energy, so you can easily stick with a single goal long enough to achieve it. And the target you pick is nearly always one that will feel good when you attain it. What's more, your self-imposed goals tend to reflect your deep-seated desires, interests, and abilities. Even if your head doesn't know what it wants, some part of you is alert enough to select self-imposed goals that motivate you the most.

A self-imposed goal is also likely to contain an attractive package of secondary motivators, the kind you miss on routine, externally imposed assignments, say, the prestige you want, the influence you crave, and the good feelings you experience by doing something useful. These secondary motivators are less related to the final aim than to the process of reaching toward that aim. They make the work itself a motivating activity.

Self-imposed goals are so powerful you can "turn up the throttle" on your own achievements simply by adjusting your goals. There is a simple and direct relationship between your goals and your achievements. Set them effectively and you will become more effective. Allow them to be set for you and you will place the direction of your work and your life in other people's hands. Of course, just setting a goal does not guarantee you will achieve it. But it does guarantee you are moving in the right direction. Later on, we'll work on the techniques to boost your performance toward the maximum; they are your best guarantee of achievement. But before you can achieve, you must first understand the importance of goals you set for yourself, and must start the process of goal setting in your own life.

SETTING YOUR OWN GOALS

Setting goals is one of the most difficult responsibilities anyone can assume—not because the goals are so hard to establish, but because so few of us take the time or trouble to ask ourselves where we are headed and what changes in direction we might prefer. All it takes to begin setting your own goals is to clarify your thoughts and feelings and work them out to their logical conclusions. Start with a simple question: "If I had more time, what would I do with it?"

In your personal notebook, list all the uses to which you could put your extra time. Don't hold anything back. After all, no one has to see this list except you; in fact, you can tear it up when you're through. Promise yourself anything that makes you feel comfortable. You'll get an extra benefit from an honest, even a slightly "offbeat" list. Putting every thought onto the paper enables you to express your more hidden desires and secret urges. (I advise you to cross *off* the list everything the least bit illegal, immoral, or fattening!)

As a practical matter, it might take several sittings and several tries at the list before you can comfortably expose all your thoughts and feelings about where you would like to go and what you would like to do. At first, you may censor the list before it hits paper. But try to fight that internal censor. You'll win if you persevere.

The idea is to begin looking as deeply as you can into your hidden dreams about the future. But since this is difficult to do without practice, it's fruitful to start by asking concrete questions about specific amounts of free time you will soon have.

Use Experience 6 as a beginning guide to looking inward at your dreams and desires. Work on it now for a few minutes, before you go on with this book.

Experience 6

If You Had More Time, What Would You Do with It?

Instructions: In your personal notebook, list the answers to each of the questions below. *Be specific!*

1) What would you do with one extra hour per week?
2) What would you do with five extra hours per week?
3) What would you do with one extra day per week?
4) What would you do with one extra week per year?

Looking for Continuity in Your Goals

The basic method of establishing goals is to look over the list you put together in answer to Experience 6. Group similar ideas, then distill your wild ideas and impractical dreams into concrete, desirable, positive goals you can reasonably expect to achieve. This process takes practice, of course, but it gets much easier after a few tries.

As you begin to spot some viable goals for yourself, you'll probably notice they have a certain familiarity. For example, one man

I know went through Experience 6 and set himself the personal goal of learning to play chess at a comfortably high level of excellence. Later, he remembered having been in the chess club in high school and having had a youthful affection for the game. His feelings for the game and the satisfaction he received from playing it well had been buried for more than twenty years. But once revived, they were as strong as ever.

In another situation, a lawyer found that this goal-setting exercise triggered a decision to emphasize a certain part of his current practice (specifically, defending doctors in malpractice cases). This was an area of law he had always enjoyed, but one that he had neglected under the pressures of building his practice. Now reminded of his interest, he made the decision to commit time and energy to acquiring skill and experience in this area. Over the years, he managed to expand his practice—and his income—while greatly increasing the satisfaction he derived from his everyday work.

Finding Your Mission

I find the best way to visualize, organize, and decide on my goals is to think in terms of my "mission." A military concept, "mission" connotes a degree of seriousness and dedication that overuse has washed out of the word "goals." "Mission" also implies importance, and your goals should be important—at least to you. Although the words are often used interchangeably, as a practical matter your mission will normally include a series of individual goals, while your goals will rarely include even one complete mission.

For example, you may have the goal of graduating from college, of earning a salary increase or promotion, of accomplishing a particularly challenging assignment, or of getting far enough ahead of your obligations to take a vacation. But your mission will be much larger. You may want to head your own strong organization, to write a satisfying novel, or to raise a happy family. Your mission will be something inspiring, something you long for, perhaps the crowning achievement of years of your life. The best missions are those that, when achieved, provide enough of an accomplishment to satisfy you for the rest of your life.

It's not as difficult as you might think to identify your mission;

the harder part is to treat your mission seriously and devote your energies to carrying it out.

Experience 6 gives you an easy first step toward finding your current mission. Go through this experience every day for a week. Answer seriously, putting down not what goals you think you should, such as "Spend more time with Mother," but the goals you truly desire, such as "Retire at age forty" or "Prove to everyone the value of my idea." Your answers are valid only if they come from your deepest feelings.

Use this Experience to learn more about yourself. Reach down into that snake pit of feelings you never, never open during the workday and see what you really want to do with your life. Didn't you have an idea a while back? Something super you thought of, you wanted to pursue, you were sure would be great if only you could iron out one or two little difficulties or get some backing or find time to work on it? Sure you did. Or if not, then you probably will soon. But before you dismiss your notion as too impractical, remember, those "impractical" ideas and aspirations are the clues you can follow until you reach a practical, satisfying, truly great idea you can and should pursue.

Such an idea may be the "pot of gold" you dare to strive for, and it may also lead you to understand and recognize your mission. What will it be? Just for fun, put down the book and spend ten minutes daydreaming or thinking about your mission. Include in your thoughts the rewards you will receive for completing it. Reflect on your list from Experience 4. Remember, your goals can tie together to form a much larger mission, or your sense of mission can help you identify and define your more immediate goals. When you have some ideas you like for your mission, come back and read on.

Translating Desires into Goals

Your first list developed from Experience 6 is not the be-all and end-all of organizing your work and life. For most of you, this is the first, tentative step in building your effectiveness. You have begun, and you will soon learn to control and shape your efforts— and through them your results. But first you must know the results you want the most. These will be your goals.

Your goals will reflect what you want from life. And this you can learn only from your list of hopes and dreams, the list you began to develop in Experience 4.

By now you've thought about what you would do with some extra time, and you've begun to connect this initial list with past interests that the pressures of your everyday life may have gradually buried.

So let's refine the initial set of Life and Career Goals from Experience 2. Take a good look at that list once again. Does it talk to you? How many of the items fire your imagination and make your blood run fast? How many of them leave you cold, your eye skipping right over the line in your hurry to look at better targets for your accomplishment? Sure, it's idealistic, but I'd like you to get to the point where every one of these goals ignites your imagination and fills your motivational cup to overflowing. You can do it.

Start by giving each of those Life and Career Goals a score from 0 to 100. Make it an overall, cosmic, what-it-is-worth-for-your-whole-life score. The more you value it, the higher the number. Sure, you'd like to double your income. Who wouldn't? But is that a goal to really make you happy, make you satisfied? Once you've doubled your income, won't you want to double it again? If so, take points away from that goal. Don't forget, you may double your income automatically as you become more effective and achieve more of the satisfying results you want. It's too early to zero in on such a narrow target.

Instead, try to give the highest points to the individual, unique, global goals you feel will absolutely make you happy, satisfied, or successful. Be careful. By mistake or by neglect, you may have less worthy targets in sight. Take the case of one business executive who is absolutely tops at financial management, who plays with large sums of money in ways almost impossible to fathom. When I asked him to state his mission, or even his immediate goals, he responded with a clear, concise set of targets for improved performance of himself and his company. So I asked him, "Tom, suppose you reach all these goals. Suppose six months or a year from now you look at this list and realize you've accomplished every single item you've put down here. Will you be happy?"

"Sure," he told me. "You asked me for my goals, and here they are."

"Right. I understand that. But will you be happy? I mean, will you be able to stop right there and count yourself lucky to have come so far and accomplished so much?"

"No way," he answered. "These are just my goals for the next year or so. I don't expect to be able to reach all of them. But even if I did, I'd be setting other goals farther out, more demanding. I'd want to do even better the next year."

This was a fine set of goals, but it failed to meet the basic criteria for a mission. As a result, Tom was a relatively unsatisfied person, despite being a top performer. I worked with Tom over a period of months, and I saw him gradually develop a sense of what he truly cared about and wanted to accomplish. Today he's a top financial decision-maker at a private university. His clear and simple mission is to keep the endowment active and generating sufficient income to meet the university's financial needs—not only for today but for decades to come. He has stepped off the treadmill of endless success and dissatisfaction. He has gained the perspective that comes from knowing one's mission, and so he's easily able to direct his efforts toward work that will bring him lifelong achievement, satisfaction, and success.

No matter what your efforts, to get the most from them you must know your mission, or at least be working to define one. Then you can begin to set yourself some goals and aim directly for what you want. Start thinking today about your mission, and don't stop until you know in your heart what it is.

In all probability, your "hopes and dreams" list from Experience 6 is a more accurate guide to your mission than your goals list from Experience 2. That's not a criticism, just an observation based on what I've seen most people write down in response to these kinds of probing questions.

You can begin to elicit your true desires and nurture them, thus defining your mission, by asking yourself the questions in Experience 6 and listening hard for the answers from deep inside yourself. Go slow with this question-and-answer session. Consider the questions often. Don't be satisfied with glib answers. In fact, don't expect to find your full, honest answers for at least a few hours, perhaps several days or a week. That's one reason to live closely with Experience 6 for a while.

Actually, your search for Life and Career Goals is an ongoing process that should always be part of you—although mostly on the back burner. Very few of us are lucky enough, as Vincent van Gogh was, to determine what we want to do, who we want to be, and what we want to accomplish with so much fervor that we need never think about these questions again. And even that great artist went through several other careers before settling on painting as his final choice of "mission."

Use Experience 7 to help define and refine your mission, and from that, your most serious goals. Remember, at this point you need not inscribe any of them in stone. You merely want to look for the goals you believe in most deeply, the goals that—if achieved today—would put you on the path toward a life's worth of effort and accomplishment. Tomorrow you'll be perfectly free to change them all around or exchange them for different goals. But in practice, you won't change them very often, because the mission you determine for yourself will be a guiding light long enough to be extremely useful.

Experience 7

Defining Your Mission

Instructions: In your personal notebook, answer the following questions to the best of your ability.

1) For what accomplishments would you like to be known after your death?

2) Who are the people whose respect for your accomplishments (past and future) means the most to you? What accomplishments would they most appreciate from you?

3) Imagine yourself ten, twenty, thirty years or more from now. You will be relaxing and evaluating what you have accomplished in your life. Which of your achievements will make you the happiest? Which ones will you regret having pursued?

4) Think about where you were, and what you were doing five, ten, or fifteen years ago. Compare those days with your present situation. Have you made progress? In what direction(s)? Do you want to continue on? Might you re-

ceive more satisfaction, pleasure, or personal reward from
some other direction(s)? Which one(s)?

WHAT TO DO WITH YOUR GOALS

I know an artist who experimented with pottery instead of his
usual oil paints and acrylics. He gave himself a year to become
acquainted with the new form. If he liked it, he would stick with
it; if not, he would go back to oils. But he made no permanent
commitment. His goal was to work steadily with clay, to give himself a fair chance for success, and then to reevaluate.

Such "experimental" personal goals are an important part of
your new program to boost your effectiveness and accomplish more
of what you want. The goals you are setting yourself today need
not become permanent choices. In most cases, a goal can prove
valuable if you retain it for at least six months or a year. During
that period, it will drive you to try new behavior, have new experiences, and perhaps gain rewards you have not experienced before.
After all this, you can make an informed decision as to whether or
not you want to keep striving for that goal. Whatever your decision, the effort and the experiences will stay with and give you a
more mature basis for additional goal setting in the future. A long-
term goal is even more valuable, provided it retains its appeal for
you. In special circumstances, even a goal you retain for less than
six months can bring you some benefit.

Setting yourself new goals is beneficial so long as they: a) reflect
your deep desires for direction and accomplishment, and b) keep
you focused and moving ahead on a relatively steady course over
a useful period of time and effort. Goals you care about and hold
on to can be very powerful. They can guide your efforts and help
you expand your results. Goals make it much easier for you to fine-
tune your efforts so they produce the most good. They also help
you discard relatively worthless activities in favor of more valuable
ones, activities whose value you may not even recognize right now.

You see, you cannot determine which activities are worth more
than others unless you have some form of yardstick to help you

measure them. And the most effective yardsticks are the goals you impose on yourself.

A Preliminary Yardstick Test

Just to give you some experience with the value of goals and the process of measuring results, let's measure today's activities against today's goals to see how effective you are at this point in your life. Later on, of course, you'll have a more detailed log of your activities and a highly refined set of goals, a combination of which gives you a far more accurate measurement. But you can get a rough measurement even without this.

Experience 8 gives you a quick method of comparing what you *planned* on doing with what you *actually* did during a given day. There are some inaccuracies in this quick look, just as there are if you look into the shiny bottom of a frying pan or a clear pool of water to see your reflection. But if this is the only mirror you have, it can still provide a revelation!

Experience 8

Planning vs. Working—A Comparison Sheet

Instructions: This is a quick inventory of what you *plan* to do versus what you *actually* do during a given day. The comparison can tell you a great deal about your current achievement problems and your potential for improvement.

1) At the beginning of your workday, list on a piece of paper everything you plan to accomplish today.
2) At the end of the same workday, list on a separate piece of paper everything you actually did today. (Use the Time Log techniques from Appendix A, if you wish.)
3) Compare: On your list of planned accomplishments, place a star next to the items you actually worked on. How many were there? Place a square next to items you actually worked on that did not appear on your list of planned accomplishments. How many were there?

4) Rate your effectiveness: Score yourself from 1 (the lowest) to 10 (the highest) on each of the following measures: How much progress did you make today toward your stated goals? What percentage of the time and effort you expended went toward achieving your stated goals?

HOW TO TELL WHAT'S USEFUL

Most people recognize only the tangible utility of an action—the immediate results they get directly from what they do. But true effectiveness can often result from actions taken to produce long-term rather than immediate results. In general, there are four Guidelines by which you can measure the utility of your actions.

Guideline 1: Active Progress Toward a Goal

This is usually the most direct form of utility, another reason goals are so important. If you have one or more desirable, well-defined goals, you can measure the usefulness of what you do quite directly. The more progress toward a goal you realize from each step you take, the more useful that step was or will be.

For example, if your goal right now is to trim excess spending from your budget, which would be more useful: a) going out and buying something you have been itching to acquire, or b) reviewing past and contemplated purchases with an eye to unnecessary or wasteful spending? I hope you answered "b." That is the more useful action because it leads more directly to your current goal.

If your current goal is to improve your results on the job, which action would be more useful: a) celebrating the occasion by taking the afternoon off to watch TV in a local bar, or b) sitting quietly and trying to decide what you would like to accomplish during the coming year? If you agree with me that "b" is the better answer, I advise you to let your actions suit your words. Do it!

Guideline 2: The Rule of Readiness

This rule is very simple: "Any action that helps you prepare to meet a future goal is as useful as direct action toward that goal."

With this rule in mind, you can make your Basic Choice of what to work on next a little more flexibly. The idea is to maximize progress toward your goals, and sometimes this means choosing not to take direct action toward a lesser goal in order to get ready for direct action toward a more important goal. For example, if you have the chance to take a dead-end job at a high rate of pay or a lower-paying job leading to opportunities you want very much, the Rule of Readiness will help you justify taking the lower-paying job. In the long run, such tactics will earn you more money, results, and satisfaction than you will probably obtain from choices that bring more immediate benefits.

Remember, the ability to achieve what you want lies not so much in the specific actions you take as in how directly what you do leads you toward your objective. And to be effective in this way requires an in-depth, enlightened self-evaluation that favors maximum goal-oriented results over the long haul.

Guideline 3: Preparation for Action

Visualize a World War II movie. It is just before the Nazis come storming over the hill, or just before the big landing on the enemy-held beach. The tension is tremendous, but there's little to do except wait. What are the movie soldiers doing? There is always that one guy worrying, crying, and complaining about the spot he's in. He's unhappy. He's concentrating on his own thoughts and fears. He's not alert to the world around him. He probably won't make it to the end of the film.

But look around. There's always another character who is quieter, calmer. He's sharpening his bayonet or oiling his machine gun. He's preparing for action. You know he has already done his best in target practice, physical conditioning, and simulated hand-to-hand combat. You can bet he has mastered the recognition signals so he won't be shot by his own buddies in case he gets separated from them. Now, with nothing to do but wait, he's honing that edge, fine-tuning his preparedness. And his thorough mental and physical preparation will make a big difference in his effectiveness. We know this character will make it to the end of the film, and probably earn a medal along the way.

Although life is not a war movie, this example is very illustrative.

Adequate preparation is vital to your effectiveness. Without it, you probably won't accomplish what you want. In business, for example, I have known managers to pore over studies and sweat their way through detailed reports, only to postpone any decision or action because a crucial bit of information was missing. All their effort and study yielded zero results, and thus *appeared* to have had no utility.

However, our Guidelines show that the work could have had a great deal of utility if, for example, the preliminary studies helped prepare the way for developing a better plan of action or for making a more accurate decision. The effort could also have been useful in another way, as described in Guideline 4.

Guideline 4: The Value of Learning

Learning experiences can often provide "utility" to gray-area efforts that may otherwise prove difficult to justify. For example, a boring, ill-planned meeting you attend may seem useless at first—but not if it teaches you to avoid such meetings in the future. In fact, if you learn anything useful, gain any good experience, or meet one helpful or stimulating person, the meeting has had at least a certain amount of utility and learning value.

Of course, if you are too generous with yourself here, you can begin valuing the learning experience of watching four hours of TV soap operas or playing fifty hands of gin rummy when you have better things to do. Don't fall into this trap. Follow your Basic Choice and work toward your most valuable goal before all others. But take a long view.

Review the results of Experience 8 again, and score your activities for utility—both long-term and short-term. Whatever the outcome, have confidence. As you learn to become more effective—better able to attain the goals and achieve the results you want—the gaps between your aims and activities will narrow. You'll find yourself able to accomplish with much greater precision and reliability whatever you set yourself to do.

GOALS YOU CAN WORK TOWARD TODAY

Now that you better realize the usefulness of goals, you can better continue the process of setting some of your own. Most people go through life without serious goals because they lack the motivation to take time and carefully set them. We don't "believe" the goals will be worth the trouble it takes to consider and select them. Why should we? For the most part, our parents were not consciously goal-setting people. And our friends and social peers don't usually interrupt the flow of talk about money, sports, and relationships to discuss their goals. We have rarely seen concrete proof that goals exist, or that having them brings any tangible reward. It's no wonder so few people are aware of their value in everyday life and work.

But it won't be fruitful for me just to order you to set goals. You won't. Instead, I must motivate you to set them. Properly motivated, you'll not only set yourself goals but—once you have them—learn firsthand their terrific and tangible value. Once I get you started, I know you won't stop. The challenge is to get you started.

So far we've had a chance to explore goals in general, and your long-term goals in particular. But the rewards from such discussions are general, and they take time to materialize. To give you more immediate motivational energy, let's turn to more immediate goals—objectives and attainments you can reach right away. But to maintain a serious and useful purpose to these goals, we'll tie them as closely as we can to some larger objective that's important to you.

Experience 9 gives you guidelines for translating a long-term goal into a series of relatively short-term and immediate steps you can start and finish in a single day. This use of one-day activities is an important standard for you to maintain. Projects that take longer often suffer from negative procrastination, declining priorities, and lack of immediate rewards. The more frequently you stick with simple steps you can start and finish in a single day, the more steadily you will progress toward your larger goals.

Experience 9

Self-Evaluation: Goals You Can Work Toward Today

Instructions: Go back in your personal notebook and review your responses to Experience 2. Use those responses as the basis for this Experience.

1) On a clean sheet in your personal notebook, list an important Life or Career Goal. Establish a reasonable deadline for achieving this goal.
2) Divide the goal into at least five smaller goals—steps or achievements you must accomplish on the road to achieving the main goal itself. For each of these five smaller goals, establish a reasonable deadline.
3) Further divide each smaller goal into several interim goals you must accomplish on the road to finishing this smaller goal. Establish a reasonable deadline for each interim goal.
4) Finally, break down each of these interim goals into one or more one-day tasks leading you toward completion of this interim step. These one-day steps become the building blocks with which you can construct a "body of work" to represent you. Put these together in any reasonable order and you're bound to accomplish a great deal. And not just any "great deal," but a specific type and style of accomplishment that spring from your own inner desires and reflect your unique interests, talents, and gifts. Almost certainly, no one else in the world could conceive of the projects you set for yourself, nor could they organize them in your special way. The same holds true of goals others set for you, but which you organize and divide into one-day tasks. Try to interest other people in doing some of the one-day tasks you've outlined in Experience 9 and you'll see how unique your contribution will be.

The one-day tasks you've just discovered lie within you—no one else. If you complete them, satisfaction and happiness await you, not only from the end results but from the very process of attempting them. In fact, reaching your goal, or doing anything that brings you closer to reaching it, is the best way to boost your effectiveness and begin obtaining the results you want from your life.

CHAPTER 3

WHAT TO DO NEXT: HOW TO DECIDE ON PRIORITIES

Organizing your work and your life, and maximizing your results, require the scientific approach: You must conscientiously and assiduously apply the general methods in this book to specific situations around you. You needn't be a true scientist, of course. You're not interested in proving a hypothesis, but in achieving your goals and objectives. Where scientists design experiments, you design strategies and tactics of accomplishment. And where scientists accumulate knowledge, you accumulate results.

"Accumulation" is the key word here. There are few opportunities for suddenly achieving tremendous results in a single day, week, or month. Oh, these opportunities do arise, and you'll soon be in a good position to create a few such opportunities and to take advantage of them when they occur. But they are relatively rare.

Much more common are the opportunities to accomplish a little extra here and there throughout the days, weeks, months, and years of your work and your life. They occur at certain key points of the day and at certain Choice Points you pass as you move from one activity to another. Each of these opportunities is of relatively little importance taken by itself. You can always afford to miss one and not look back, because another will be along very shortly. Yet without going crazy or becoming a perfectionist, the more of these opportunities you convert into extra-result realities, the better—because they accumulate very quickly.

But converting these opportunities is only part of the trick. The other part is converting them without extra effort. If you exert yourself tremendously to achieve tremendous results, you are certainly doing well. But when you develop the habits and carefully cultivated patterns of action to convert these opportunities almost effortlessly, even automatically, you can accumulate a truly huge amount of extra achievement because you won't wear yourself out prematurely.

You can think of this as a process of collecting wild daisies. Imagine you're walking with a friend in the woods where wildflowers grow along the path. If you concentrate all your energies on watching for the daisies, then picking, arranging, and counting them every few steps, you won't pay enough attention to your friend or the rest of your surroundings. The daisies—and the process of collecting them—will dominate your thoughts and block out your ability to do much else.

On the other hand, you can take the same walk through the same woods with the same friend, but this time leave the daisy collecting to take care of itself. You can probably collect the flowers "absentmindedly": stooping, picking, and holding them without special thought while you concentrate on your friend, your conversation, and the sights, smells, sounds, and textures of the forest. At the end of this walk, you will have nearly the same handful of daisies. But you won't remember picking them, nor will they have drawn much attention away from other aspects of your experience in the woods.

That's the way to convert your daily opportunities for extra results. Convert them automatically, without thought, and each little bit extra you accomplish will add to the tremendous "free bonus" you'll accumulate over the long term. The basic method for accumulating these opportunities is to identify your most valuable goals and to keep your efforts directed toward them as much as possible. With the four Guidelines of Chapter 2 in mind, you will see many, many ways to work toward your primary goals rather than other, more immediate, but less valuable objectives.

This process of concentrating your efforts toward your most important goals has two phases: The first phase requires you to:

a) Identify your most important goals
b) Map out plans to achieve them
c) Put these plans ahead of all the other items that seem to demand your time and energy

The second, equally important phase requires that you:

d) Identify your less important goals
e) Link them to the actions and efforts that will move you toward these goals
f) Consciously and deliberately refrain from these actions in favor of those in "c," above

With this two-part strategy, on one hand you devote your time to your important goals, and on the other you withhold your time from less important ones. In practice, concentrating your efforts this way on your most important goals comes down to a matter of choice. And the most common—most important—choice you can ever make with regard to organizing your work and your life, and obtaining the results you want from your efforts, is: "What am I going to do next?" This is the *Basic Choice* in your life.

You make this Basic Choice dozens of times a day. You make a Choice of "What to do next?" whenever you finish a project, hang up the telephone, start or stop a chain of thought—or even pause between activities. Your ability to accomplish what you want depends largely on how well you make these Basic Choices, even under adverse conditions: when you're not feeling well, when you're under pressure or in the midst of chaos, or when you're groping blindly in the dark.

If this were an easy task, everyone would make perfect Basic Choices all the time. But comfort yourself with this thought: You needn't build a perfect record. You are allowed ample lapses. As in baseball, where no one bats 1.000, if you just concentrate on increasing your overall percentage of fruitful Basic Choices, you'll do just fine and get plenty of good results.

Now look back at your comparison of goals and activities in Experience 8. You probably didn't do very well, but this is almost certainly because you're just starting to try. This measure of your effectiveness will now begin to improve. Make a note on your calendar to make the same comparison between current goals and actions in about two weeks, and again two weeks after that. Remember to count both the matched and the unmatched items. Your score will improve two ways: You will find your actions staying closer to your goals, and you will find you have more goals to pursue. Both are basic signs that your effectiveness is on the upswing.

THE ONE "BEST" ITEM

Once you begin to see your level of accomplishment as the sum result of your many Basic Choices—"What am I going to do next?"—a lot of abstract principles and much high-sounding philosophy suddenly solidify into concrete form.

To organize your work and your life, to achieve what you want faster and more effectively, begin noticing how often the Basic Choice presents itself. Make your Basic Choices in support of your most important goals. And get into the habit of scrutinizing your options to find the best Choice possible, as often as you can.

You can begin by paying attention to how often the Basic Choice occurs in your life. For example, mentally review your activities today. Use Experience 10 to help you recall some crucial Basic Choices and how well you converted them to extra results.

Experience 10

Reviewing Your Basic Choices

Instructions: Take a few moments and think about what you did today. What did you plan? What did you work toward and accomplish?

1)   In your personal notebook, list the very first things you did when you woke up this morning. Then list five other things you could have done instead.
2)   List three goals you actively pursued between breakfast

and lunch today. Then list five other goals you could have pursued. Mark each one with a " + " or a " − " to indicate whether it is more or less important than any goal you actually worked toward.

3) List three goals you actively pursued between lunch and dinner today. Then list five other goals you could have pursued. Mark each one with a " + " or a " − " to indicate whether it is more or less important than any goal you actually worked toward.

4) List three goals you actively pursued between dinner and bedtime today. Then list five other goals you could have pursued. Mark each one with a " + " or a " − " to indicate whether it is more or less important than any goal you actually worked toward.

5) Go back through each list and write down (merely explaining to yourself in your head won't benefit you) why you made the Basic Choice to work toward the goals you actively pursued.

The questions in Experience 10 are designed to elicit from you a random sample of the reasons you work toward whatever goals and objectives you select. I suspect you have not been aware of most of these reasons before this. In other words, you may have to sit and think a spell before you can write down a solid reason for making whatever Basic Choices you do.

That's all to the good because your untrained mind probably makes poor Basic Choices right now. Later on, both your conscious and your unconscious selves will be superbly trained to handle your Choices accurately and effectively. You'll be choosing "automatically," picking those daisies without taking any attention away from the people and the situations around you. For now, though, you'll be more effective if you pay strict attention to where you direct your efforts. By watching what you do, and later by trying to direct your efforts in carefully planned patterns, you'll almost instantly increase your level of results and the amount of satisfaction you can generate in a day.

Of course, it's tedious to pay attention to your Basic Choices, just as it would be tedious to pay much attention to the simple act of running. Most of us just run. But think of this as a special form of running. It is more like running a long-distance event—every day for the rest of your life. For you to succeed at such an event, your every movement becomes extremely important. The slightest flaw in your running style can hamper your efforts, waste precious energy, and ultimately slow you down. Similarly, slight flaws in the ways you make your Basic Choices will ultimately reduce your effectiveness and hamper your efforts to achieve what you want. For now, pay attention to detail.

Eventually, you will get the knack for making the best Choice almost without thinking. For example, I'm working and the telephone rings. It is someone calling to discuss one aspect of another project I'm involved in. Instinctively, I ask questions to determine if I must talk about this right now. As in most situations, there is some flexibility. Next, I use my personal criteria and guidelines to measure the importance of this new item in relation to the one I'm currently pursuing. Even before the caller can begin detailing the reason he or she called, I hear my voice saying, "Listen, I'm right in the middle of something else right now. Can we talk about this later?"

It's easy to make an appointment to discuss the matter two days from now, far enough away that I can factor it into my schedule. Even putting off this new conversation for a single hour will enable me to reach a natural break point in my current work, and thus avoid an interruption that interferes with my thinking and lowers my overall effectiveness.

At a different time, however, I might receive the same call and elect to drop what I'm doing and cover the caller's topic at length. Why? Because a moment spent considering my Basic Choice convinces me this telephone "interruption" will help me achieve a more important goal than the one I was working toward when the phone rang.

With a little practice, it becomes very easy, almost instinctive, to keep forging and revamping your schedule in order to pursue your most important goals and thus to maximize the results of your efforts. But in the beginning you can benefit from having some of the rules and criteria carefully laid out. As you assimilate them and incorporate them into your pattern of work and life, you'll spend less and less brainpower putting these ideas to use. Eventually, you will use them automatically. I guarantee it.

TWO TEASERS

Which is the more valuable effort?

a) Listening to your child tell you excitedly about something inconsequential that went on at school today?
b) Hearing on the telephone what the garage mechanic has to say about your car's broken starter?

Which is the more "important" responsibility?

a) Tackling that amazingly difficult report your boss threw at you yesterday and demanded back completed by 5 P.M. today?
b) Making an effort to contact that "special someone" you met last night?

Before we get to specific criteria, let's examine the concept of the one "best" item for you to work on. Again, it's not a narrow, rigid construction that dictates all your actions or raises tangible results above long-term, less concrete values and benefits. Too many people use "effectiveness" and the quest for maximum results as excuses for neglecting people or ignoring important emotional and social aspects of their work and their lives. They wind up acting more like machines than people. This is not the "best" course for you to follow.

The idea of there being one "best" item to absorb your efforts at any given moment seems to suggest that you use some kind of objective accounting procedure to keep track of your options and put them in rank order. But in practice it would be absurd to begin trying to compare and rank such disparate demands as:

• Your kids
• Your current love affair
• A consuming interest in a new topic
• A long-term marriage option

- A broken car
- An impending deadline at work

They all demand your attention, and it's impossible to put accurate numbers on these items and rank them "objectively."

At any given moment, your options for directing your efforts form a dazzling array of the practical and the fantastic, the must-do and the should-do, the interesting and the deadly dull. So how, then, to know which of all your options is the one "best" for you to pursue?

"BEST" DEPENDS ON WHEN YOU CHOOSE

To make life practical, you must limit your Basic Choices to a few appropriate options. Instead of considering every possibility at every opportunity, keep your Choice among the most relevant options that fit with your priority at the moment.

Divide your life and work into several Periods of Priority. During working hours, for example, you already tend to limit your consideration of "What to do next?" to work-related objectives and goals. Your one "best" option during working hours is, quite naturally, different from your one "best" option in the shopping mall or at home Your best option for lunch differs from your best option just a few minutes earlier or later. Apply this idea to simplify all your Basic Choices. Ignore (or give less consideration to) certain options in favor of more appropriate goals and activities. During a Saturday afternoon, for example, your Basic Choice can be limited to career-advancing studies, while during weekday evenings you can choose solely from a number of family-oriented or enjoyable opportunities. By focusing on a small, appropriate list of options, you greatly simplify your Basic Choice of "What to do next?"

You can get more practical benefits from this concept by clearly reserving whatever Periods of Priority make sense to you. Define what hours of the day and what days of the week you will be primarily concerned with your work. For most of us, that's from 9 A.M. through 5 P.M. Monday through Friday. Others will establish different hours in which work takes top priority.

Then reserve other Periods of Priority: for family and friends;

for sports, exercise, or hobbies; for socializing and entertainment; for home-maintenance jobs like shopping, repairs, cooking, cleaning, and laundry; for mental exercises, meditation, reading, or study; even for self-improvement through whatever means appeal to you.

The main purpose of defining your Periods of Priority is to simplify your Basic Choices during each Period by ruling out the vast majority of all the items you could possibly tackle next.

"BEST" DEPENDS ON YOUR MOOD

In addition to Periods of Priority, there is the factor of plain and simple saturation. Imagine that you love working in your garden, for example. Your Choice of "What to do next?" leads you to spend half a dozen hours there during the first two or three days of the week. Fine. But now you begin to feel you have gardened enough. For the moment, you don't want to do it anymore: you are saturated with gardening. And so you temporarily block off gardening from consideration when you wonder "What to do next?" Saturation makes your Basic Choices simpler. It works almost like a *negative priority,* such as: "No matter what, I'm not gardening for a while."

The gardening example illustrates a negative urge, but you may also feel positive urges you want to pursue. For example, no matter what, you want to watch TV. No matter what, you want to eat some pizza. Most of the time, positive urges quickly lead to saturation, which leads in turn to negative urges until you're balanced once again.

"BEST" DEPENDS ON EXTERNALS

Your environment also helps limit your Basic Choice, in both favorable and unfavorable ways. For example, at social gatherings you don't generally work out mathematical models or practice your hobby of duck calls. Instead, you respond to your environment and converse with the people around you. You don't read heavy philosophy at amusement parks; you go on simpleminded rides. In the country, you admire the trees, the sky, and the smell of good, clean air rather than go looking for a nightclub or a stock exchange. Appropriately limiting your Basic Choices to fit your present environment helps you quickly identify the most productive and satisfying course of action.

A COMPREHENSIVE CHOICE

Your Basic Choice of "What to do next?" should result in a selection that best suits all your emotional, spiritual, physical, financial, and other needs of the moment, along with your ongoing needs for Utility and Goal Orientation.

But in pursuing this comprehensive ideal, we are not automatons blindly throwing our available energies into the most practical project available. Rather, we are holistic human beings who cultivate both short-term and long-term values with a balanced program of activities that serve all our needs. We want to develop new goals as well as attain our current ones.

In all you do, stay aware of your total human self. You are not merely a producer, not merely a consumer, not merely an achiever or a worker. You must learn to achieve what you want not only to accumulate wealth and power but to earn greater satisfaction and leave a better world for those who follow.

It takes practice to learn to make these Choices and to reach all your goals most effectively. Starting now, and continuing well after you finish reading this book, I want you to practice, evaluate, and attempt to control your efforts and your achievements. Experience 11 is designed to help you think about the range of Choices available in your current situations.

Experience 11

Self-Evaluation: Choosing Tomorrow's Achievements

Instructions: Take a few moments and think about tomorrow. What have you planned? What are you going to work toward and accomplish?

1)   In your personal notebook, list the projects, tasks, hob-

bies, or "general agenda" items you expect to pursue tomorrow. How many items can you list? Rank the items in
two sets: first, the items you consider to be of "major" importance; and separately, the items you consider to be of
"minor" importance.

2)   For each "major" item, list at least one other project, task,
      hobby, or "general agenda" item you could pursue in its
      place. Try to emphasize items that best reflect your stated
      goals and objectives.

3)   For each "minor" item, list at least one other project,
      task, hobby, or "general agenda" item you could pursue in
      its place.

4)   Go through these lists and select the items you will actu-
      ally pursue tomorrow. Make sure you select only as many
      as you can reasonably handle. Beside each item you will
      pursue tomorrow, briefly note why you decided to pursue
      it at this time.

URGENCY IN A BASIC CHOICE

Another element to consider in your Basic Choice is an item's
urgency. Urgency is a dangerous factor. It requires steady nerves
and good judgment to discriminate true urgency from all the ap-
parent urgency with which trivial problems often cloak themselves.
Yet such nerves and judgment are important to cultivate if you are
going to improve your effectiveness and achieve more of what you
want. In addition, people will frequently put urgent tasks ahead of
more important ones, despite their knowledge that urgency is no
clue to the importance of a task, a goal, or an anticipated result.

For example, say your goal is to write an opera by age thirty-
five. This is not urgent until well after your thirty-fourth birthday.
But by then it's too late! You missed achieving this goal, despite
how important you felt it to be.

Focusing on urgency alone will cause you to ignore consistently
the long-range projects that require training, momentum, confidence, and experience. Yet these Choices are the ones that can bring
you the most satisfying results. If you focus on urgency, you'll
emphasize rapid-fire details over slower, more meaningful achieve-

ments. You won't get what you want, whether that is to write operas, to run a small business, to find a better job, or to complete any project that requires initiative and good planning.

Urgency can be an important factor, though, as a tiebreaker when the motivations behind the rest of your Choices are well balanced. In making a Basic Choice where all your options seem about equal, it's easy and natural to pick the most urgent. But when a more urgent task is clearly less valuable than another option, it takes courage and self-discipline to select the less urgent/more important option.

For example, imagine you have just finished work on an item and you are now considering your next Basic Choice. Your options include:

a) Reading a current journal
b) Returning a phone call from a stranger
c) Handling an urgent problem before your bank closes
d) Thinking about your day and what you would like to accomplish

Reading a current journal is an important task, but probably not an urgent one. Whether or not you choose to do this now depends on what else is currently on your plate.

Returning a phone call from a stranger is not important enough to take priority over anything with obvious value or urgency.

The banking problem may be a valid one, but its urgency may be a mirage. If you can call the bank after closing time, or handle the problem in a letter, you have no real reason to put that item ahead of others more important.

Thinking about your day and what you would like to accomplish is probably the most important activity on this list. It has hidden urgency, too, because the sooner you do this work, the more impact it will have on your productivity for the rest of the day.

Basic Choices are fundamental but not easy. The ideal is to make your Basic Choice in favor of the one activity that moves you furthest toward an important goal. If the right task does not appear obvious at first, you can take time to consider your plans and break them into smaller tasks. It will be easier to compare these and choose among them. Soon you'll be able to initiate your own goal-

oriented tasks instead of blindly obeying the summons of less important alternatives that scream out for attention.

But talking about Basic Choices won't help you. This process is
best learned by making Basic Choices—and by making more and
more of them until you have the habit of putting your shoulder
not just to the next available wheel but to the one wheel that best
promotes and supports your larger goals and purposes.

Experience 12 will help guide your thinking as you try to decide
how to make Basic Choices for improving your results and accomplishing more of what you want.

Experience 12

Self-Evaluation: Making the Basic Choice

Instructions: Use this Experience to help you choose between alternatives that seem to have equal claims upon your attention and
effort. On closer inspection, you will probably find that one
alternative has a stronger claim, based on what you want to
accomplish and how you plan to proceed. Use these questions
to start probing for that one most important opportunity to
improve your results.

1) In your personal notebook, write down everything you
    might reasonably select as your next activity at work or at
    home.
2) For each option, list the potential results you might
    achieve, and the probability you can achieve them.
3) For each option, rank from 1 (least) to 5 (most) how di-
    rectly it leads you toward one of your major goals.
4) For each option, rank its degree of urgency from 1 (least)
    to 5 (most). Also note the likely results if you do not pur-
    sue it at this time.

5) Which option seems to offer you the most rewards or potential rewards right now?

Play to Your Strengths

Don't forget to factor into your Basic Choices some of your own strengths and weaknesses, too. As you'll discover in forthcoming chapters, your effectiveness goes up when you work more often on what you do best. So the best answer to your Basic Choice will at least partly depend on your current strengths and weaknesses. The more accurately you recognize them, the more of your effort you can direct toward achieving your best objectives.

For example, unless you have special training, you may be better off having a tax professional do your tax-related paperwork, and having other specialists handle other parts of your paperwork. Admit this, and let them do the work! In general, subordinates, colleagues, outside consultants, and professionals can take a huge burden of less demanding or more specialized work from your shoulders. Let them. And then direct the energy and effort you have set free toward projects and objectives only you can achieve.

ACQUIRING THE INTUITIVE KNACK

By now you are probably feeling overburdened by all the factors you must consider every time you make a Basic Choice. If you're like most people on their first exposure to these ideas, you can't even keep them all straight. You certainly have trouble balancing every factor that bears on your Basic Choice. And to do all this figuring and balancing quickly seems just about impossible.

There is a trick you can use here, though, to "program" all this material into your subconscious mind. Once you program it, the right half of your brain automatically considers "What to do next?"—leaving your conscious, achieving, workaday half relatively free to concentrate on the task itself with maximum energy and minimum fuss. Putting your Basic Choices under control of your "other half" is by far the best way to handle them. Otherwise, you work harder pondering what to do than doing it.

Here is a simple four-step process for turning your Basic Choices over to the quiet side of your brain:

Step 1: Read pages 34–47 of this book in one sitting, straight through from beginning to end. While you're reading, make notes on the material in your personal notebook. If any questions pop up about how to handle specific situations, formulate answers that satisfy you. Try to understand the information as a cohesive unit. You may not succeed the first time, but try. Go over the material again every three days until you feel you understand how all the factors fit and work together in your own special situation.

Step 2: After each reading, put down the book and for a few minutes try to imagine yourself using this information to make your Basic Choices instantly and accurately. Absorb the feelings, the benefits, the accomplishments your new mastery will generate. Will it reduce tensions? Smooth the flow of work? Help you achieve lifelong goals? Be specific about the benefits you expect.

Step 3: Try to be more conscious of your Basic Choices as you make them. First, simply notice each Choice Point. Then, begin to identify your options and why you selected the one you did. Don't fret or spend long minutes on each Basic Choice. Simply recognize it, make it, and follow what you choose.

Step 4: Once or twice a day, look back at your Basic Choices. How well did your choices turn out? This review helps program the process of making Basic Choices into your mind. As you review, consider the goals and objectives you have and have not pursued most recently. Notice any improvements. Then continue with the program.

Over a period of several weeks and months, you'll begin integrating more of the important factors smoothly into your Basic Choices. And you'll make each Choice a little faster, a little better, a little more confidently than before. Soon the entire process will be so automatic and intuitive that you will almost feel as though the one "best" alternative for action leaps out at you of its own free will.

"What Choice?" you'll soon be saying. "I had no Choice. There was only one 'best' thing to do, and I did it!"

CHAPTER 4

SPECIFIC
TECHNIQUES FOR
ACCOMPLISHING
MORE IN
LESS TIME

Effectiveness, satisfaction, and accomplishment all depend on obtaining desirable results. In this chapter, you'll find many specific techniques for obtaining more results faster, smoother, and more effortlessly than you ever thought possible. Not all the techniques apply to every task or every situation, but those that do can become an integral part of your effort to shape your results and to make the best possible use of your time, your energy, and your resources.

You already investigated the *philosophical* aspects of effectiveness when you zeroed in on your life and career goals: among all things possible, picking those few you wanted to achieve. The *managerial,* or *executive,* aspects came up when you faced your Basic Choice: "What am I going to do next?" There the object was to stimulate your leadership qualities—even if you ended up leading only yourself.

Now we're working on the *technical,* or *practical,* aspects of effectiveness, concerned solely with how we can move quickly along the road that our *executive* selves have chosen as the best way toward the objectives our *philosophical* selves have designated.

HANDLING ALL YOUR PAPER

Forms, letters, memos, reports—items to be filled in, read, analyzed, written, and talked about—flood our lives. Paperwork is a well-recognized problem, but very few of us do very much to solve it. Unless you have a clerical job sorting, filing, retrieving, or otherwise handling paper, your paperwork is more of a means to an end than an end in itself; therefore, it should not take over or dominate your time.

If you are now—or ever will be—in a position of organizational or bureaucratic influence, I urge you to do what you can to eliminate unnecessary paperwork, to streamline what is necessary, and to keep all of it in its proper place.

In the meantime, let's see what we can do about your particular pile of paperwork.

UNNECESSARY PILES

Most of us tend to pile papers around us, on the desk, the credenza, the top of the filing cabinet, the coffee table, the floor—anywhere there's a horizontal surface. This is so true I can often estimate people's ability to cope with their situation by glancing at the piles of paperwork visible in their home or office.

A profusion of paper indicates to me a serious problem. An occasional pile shows me you need some help, but that your case is not critical. One accountant I know has covered every horizontal surface in his office, not with one but with multiple piles! That's right! A bottom pile about six inches thick, bound in a rubber band or made up of uniform-size papers. Then on top, another pile bound in a separate rubber band or made up of a different type of paper. Sometimes, one pile is bridged across two others; in several cases, the piles are three or four units high. Some of them are UPOs—Unidentified Piled Objects. The man no longer knows or cares what is in them.

If you love your paper piles—if you have some psychological

need to retain your paperwork longer than it retains its value—I'm going to have a hard time helping you out of that habit. You may need an entirely different kind of help.

But if your habit has developed out of neglect or lack of training, or if you honestly feel having those papers "right at your fingertips" helps you work more effectively, you can be helped, and right now!

The truth is, those piles are nothing but millstones around your neck. Face it! They don't help you work more effectively, any more than piles of old junky car parts help your garage mechanic do his job any faster or better. My grandfather used to save old calendars. He'd say, "If that year ever comes back, Rob, I'm going to be ready!" I guess it was a joke. But it was no joke living with a pile of musty, rolled-up calendars, waiting for 1943 to return.

Look at your various piles. Then look at the facts. How many of those papers will actually prove useful to you? If you are anything like the people I've helped break the pile habit, about 75 percent of that stuff is junk. You'll never look at it, except in the course of searching for something else. You'll never miss it when it's gone. And while you're hoarding old annual reports and last month's reading matter, you're letting those papers get in the way of today's shot at greater effectiveness.

THE MEASLES SYNDROME

So don't believe me. But use a trick I call the Measles Syndrome to spot your own problem of unwanted, unnecessary, and useless piles of paper.

From now on, every time you turn to one of them to look for something you need, carry a pencil or a fine-line marker with you. Put a light dot in one corner of every document you touch as you work through the pile. Put another dot in the same place the next time you sort past that document looking for something else.

Just for fun, write down your guess as to how many times you will handle the top sheet of each pile: I'm willing to bet your guess is much too low.

In a very short time, your paper piles will break out in "measles." You'll have more dots than you can shake a stick at. By some counts, some people handle a single piece of paper 135 times or more while it sits in a pile on their desk! And then it's still in the way! So start counting the number of times you handle those papers in the course of looking for something to work on. Once you're convinced the piles subtract from your effectiveness, you can take remedial action.

CLEARING AWAY OBSTRUCTIONS

Try to get in the habit of working with an absolutely clear desk. The only useful papers on your desk are those that pertain to the one "most important" item on which you are working. Put everything else away.

"Out of sight, out of mind" applies here in a very literal sense. Most people keep papers in plain sight at least partly so they won't forget the matters to which the papers refer. They're afraid if they file a particular paper away, the task or responsibility it represents will fade from their consciousness, with suitably awful consequences.

They may be right. But that's not a valid excuse for overburdening your desk. You don't have to live with your relatives to remember who they are, do you? Why believe you must constantly view all your paperwork to keep it in mind?

What actually happens is that your piles of paper make it harder to concentrate on that one "most important" task. Every time your eyes stray around your desk, or anywhere you have piles, your mind is wrenched off track by the memory of some other important item facing you. That your memory can be aided by visual reminders is valuable to know, because you can use this trick selectively to jog your memory regarding certain important items you want to keep in mind. But the key word is "selectively." When you use it too often, this trick becomes counterproductive.

In fact, you come to resemble an overworked salesman at a convention. You start talking to one potential customer. But just as you reach a crucial point in the sales process, you spot someone else who is fingering your merchandise. So you rush off to make a sale there. But before you get the signature on the order form, a third prospect grabs your sleeve and asks a hard question about a different item. In the middle of your answer, you remember a great sales point you should have told a previous prospect, so you drop everything to make a quick phone call to get this point across before you forget it. But while you're waiting for that person to come on the line, someone new enters your sales booth and wants to talk with you, too.

By the end of the day, you've been busy! You've spoken to hundreds of prospects. But you haven't completed a single sale. Net score: zero!

This kind of Ping-Pong approach to accomplishment—played with half a dozen paddles instead of just two—is a guaranteed way to lose control of your time, your energy, and your efforts. When you surround yourself with those 8½-by-11-inch invitations to digress, you're asking for ineffectiveness. And you're going to get it.

The better alternative is to keep a clear desk. Put those papers out of sight, and let them stay out of your mind while you concentrate on your one "most important" project. And don't worry about forgetting what to work on next. You won't! In the next few pages, you'll see a variety of tips and techniques that guarantee you'll never lose track of your projects, or your paperwork, while keeping a clean desk and an orderly, highly prioritized flow of work.

As a practical matter, you will certainly remember the most important items on your agenda. For a variety of reasons, these items will come to mind every time you face your Basic Choice of "What to do next?"

In addition, you'll learn some very effective mnemonic techniques that will keep your agenda items in front of you without letting them block your forward progress.

For example, you'll soon be in the habit of maintaining a written daily plan. This little slip of paper will take the place of your most relevant piles of paperwork—without their bulk and the unwanted way they grab at your attention. You'll read more about this idea later in this chapter.

Seven Steps to Tame the Paper Dragon

Paperwork is not a unified problem. There are several different types of paperwork, which is why it takes seven different methods to handle it all. In the next few pages, we'll detail all the elements of a comprehensive paperwork system, as well as show you how they go together to simplify your work and life and improve your productivity.

1) THE DAILY PROMPTER

TV personalities face the camera armed with a variety of memory aids to help them keep track of what to say and do. Why should you suffer with any less?

The Daily Prompter (also called the "ticker" file or the "bring forward" file) is a fancy name for a common device nearly all people have used at one time or another to jog their memories and help them keep track of many details. Every time you note a doctor's appointment on a kitchen calendar, for example, you're setting up a one-day "prompt." The calendar itself is a kind of prompter, and it works very well if you will only use it. The only drawbacks to your kitchen or office calendar are: a) it is probably too small for you to note in full detail all the information you want to put in your Daily Prompter, and b) it has no place to store anything bulkier than a brief, written message.

A Daily Prompter file is a much more useful device because it never goes out of date and you can have one with as large a capacity as you will ever need.

Physically, your Daily Prompter can be a series of large envelopes, files, hanging file folders, accordion files, binders, drawers, or boxes. For twelve months and thirty-one days, you need forty-three containers or separate storage spaces in all. Number them from 1 to 31, and put the names of the twelve calendar months on the remainder.

In action, the Daily Prompter is the one place to store—and hence retrieve—all sorts of messages, paperwork, and information you want to remember but don't want to (or are afraid you may not be able to) hold in your brain until needed.

Note that:

a) Your Daily Prompter is only as useful as the information you put into it. Get in the habit of filing everything that:
   1) you are holding, thinking about, or doing now, and
   2) you will want to notice again sometime in the future.
b) Your Daily Prompter is useful only if you rely on it. Get in the habit of going to it first thing every morning to see what you have filed for yourself under today's date.

c) Your Daily Prompter can help you in your personal life as well as your work. You can mix messages in a single file, if you wish, but you may prefer to establish two different Daily Prompters and use them both: one for personal-life matters, one for your career.

For example, if you make an appointment for a shampoo, cut, and blow-dry next Thursday, drop yourself a note about the appointment (or a business card may be enough by itself) in your Daily Prompter for next Thursday's date. If the appointment is very early Thursday morning, you may want to leave the reminder in Wednesday's container, then move it to Thursday's when it first comes up to remind you.

Or suppose you have a car payment to make on the twenty-fifth of every month. Put your payment book, or something to remind you of the payment coming due, in your Daily Prompter sometime before the twenty-fifth—early enough so you can make the payment on time. Leave it there from month to month. So long as you check your Daily Prompter, you'll never miss a payment.

Now suppose you have a meeting to attend on the eighth of the month and you want to bring some important papers with you. Drop the papers, clipped to a note about the meeting (where, when, who, what, why), in folder 8. Sure, you may forget about the meeting and lose track of where you put its paperwork, but if you only remember to check your Daily Prompter every morning, the paperwork and meeting reminder will appear when you need them. If you must do some preparation for the meeting, leave the note and paperwork in folder 7, 6, or even an earlier one.

Now you can see why you don't need piles of paperwork on your desk just so you won't forget something. Put those papers in your general filing system (more details on this system coming soon), then drop yourself a note under the appropriate date in your Daily Prompter telling yourself where you put the papers and what you want to do with them. You can then forget them, supremely confident in your knowledge that—like Moby Dick—your paperwork will rise again to beckon you on the appropriate date, and no sooner.

You can leave notes and other items you want to see far in the future under the appropriate months. Then on the first day of each month, open that month's file and put the items into the appropriate daily files accordingly to the dates you need them.

One thing I love about the Daily Prompter is how a small amount of energy expended to file items and check today's folder in the morning pays huge dividends out of all proportion to your investment. You get peace of mind from knowing you won't forget anything; you get the use of the mental energy released from no longer having to remember—it's now available for other work; you get the convenience of having your appointments, ideas, and paperwork automatically leap into your hand at just the appropriate time; and you get the added effectiveness derived from keeping your commitments, not forgetting items, and clearing your desk.

The Daily Prompter is also a great way to keep tabs on your own activities and progress. For example, say you get the idea to begin reading books by Henry Miller, or to take a friend fly-fishing in Montana, or to sign up for a Cordon Bleu cooking course. Leave yourself a note in the Daily Prompter a month or two into the future. When the note pops up, you are reminded of what you were thinking and hoping to accomplish. Either you have done it or you haven't; either you still want to or you don't. Whatever the current picture, you get a strong sense of how you are changing or staying the same during a period far longer than your usual span of recollection. And this may get you moving toward new projects and goals.

The Daily Prompter is one way to keep up correspondence with friends and colleagues. Instead of setting down their letters (perhaps to be lost forever amid your paper piles) with a vague intention of writing back—someday—you put the letter purposefully into your Daily Prompter. When it comes up again, make a point of writing—or calling—to keep in touch. This greatly improves your ability to maintain contact, despite a busy schedule.

Your Daily Prompter is a valuable tool in your efforts to make better decisions. It can curb impulse buying and give maturity to your judgments. For example, suppose you get a mailing piece urging you to buy a videotape recorder for only $999 and you very much want to send away for it. Go ahead—fill in the order form and address the envelope. Then put the whole package into your Daily Prompter for a week or so from today. When it comes up, look it over again. You may not find the offer so attractive this time around. But if you do, you can send for it with more confidence your decision is a good one.

Or suppose someone asks for your opinion or judgment on a weighty matter. Instead of responding off the top of your head, do your thinking and formulate your answer—for your eyes only. Put the question and your answer into your Daily Prompter overnight, or longer if possible. When it comes out again, you have a chance to reevaluate your previous judgment, almost as if it belonged to someone else. You will be surprised how many foolish, hasty, or superficial judgments you will be able to keep to yourself by this means.

As you become more comfortable with your Daily Prompter, you'll find many other uses for this simple but effective tool.

2) THE COMPREHENSIVE FILING SYSTEM

Most people start their paper piles innocently enough, but once started, the little darlings tend to grow and grow until they are out of control and you can't find what you want without a lengthy search. I have noticed most piles start for one of two excuses (I won't dignify them with the label "reasons"): a) "There's no place else to put this for now," and b) "I'm just going to leave it here for a short while."

If you cut off these excuses at the roots, your unwanted paper piles won't have as much chance to grow. Two good ways to keep them from growing are: a) have a good place—preferably only one good place—for everything you conceivably might want to retain, and b) keep everything in its place—and therefore not on your desk—except during those moments you are actively working on it.

A Comprehensive Filing System is the masterstroke here. It gives you a place—with adequate space—for all your paperwork. And more, it gives you confidence you can find whatever you file whenever you want it again. That's a big psychological factor when it comes time to put your paperwork out of sight.

Let's face it: A messy filing system is like a messy closet. You must take everything out to find what you want. And every once in a while, you open the door and the whole thing collapses in your face. No wonder you don't like to use it very often, and prefer to keep everything in piles all around you.

But a well-organized filing system, with room for everything you are likely to store there, is an open invitation to clear your work space and concentrate on one task. In fact, it's almost an indispensable tool for deep concentration and total effectiveness.

It's important to have enough good storage places for paper related to ongoing activities, programs, and projects. Every "thing" you are currently working on or thinking about should be represented with its own folder or file. In fact, I start a new folder as soon as I see I might refer to an idea or some information more than two or three times. I keep these files organized according to how I think of the information they contain. For example, if I think of several people or items under one general category, I'll file them all in one folder. But if I think of the same items as separate but related, I'll file them in individual folders with cross-referencing notes, or I'll put the folders physically together.

I don't stick with a rigid formula, but I do like my filing system to reflect my mental categories and my natural patterns of thought. For example, I often give complex projects several subdivision folders within a larger hanging file to facilitate better retrieval. I occasionally group other projects into a single folder, particularly if I rarely work with these papers. I keep all my "current activities" in strict alphabetic order.

I won't prescribe any hard-and-fast rules for you. As I said, to be useful a work file like this must be tied to your personal thought patterns and working habits. However, consider starting a new folder whenever: a) you feel as if you need it, b) you have just spent more than three minutes finding a specific item in your files, or c) you want to file an item that doesn't quite fit into any existing slot or category. (If you keep your own files, organize them to reflect the way you think. If you have a secretary or assistant to keep your files, establish a standardized filing system that everyone can easily follow.)

File folders, supplies, and equipment are cheap when compared with the cost of the time you waste searching for items you grouped too closely or too generally.

CROSS-REFERENCING

The biggest problem with these individual files is that sometimes a single bit of information or a whole package of paperwork really belongs with two or three other files. The logical solution is to make duplicates and file the whole package everywhere it belongs. But then you have the problem of updating the duplicates, and you end up with a very bulky filing system. It's usually faster, cheaper, and easier to use cross-reference slips. Before you file the multiple-interest item, think of all the key words by which you might look for it later. Then make and file cross-reference slips under each key word, referring you to the file's actual location.

For example, imagine that a colleague approaches me with a proposal for a brand-new publication. Because it's his baby, I want to keep the paperwork with other items under his name. Because it's a good idea for a publication, I want it filed with other good ideas for future reference. The proposal is so far along that it really deserves a file of its own. And because I promised to reply to him within two weeks, I need a reminder of it in my Daily Prompter. I resolve the problem of where to put the paperwork by using cross-reference forms (original plus—in this case—two copies).

I put the actual paperwork regarding the proposal into its own project file. Each cross-reference form lists all the key words: my colleague's name, the publication idea, the date the response is due, and the name of the proposed publication. I circle the name of the proposed publication to show myself where I put the actual paperwork. Then I slip the cross-reference forms into each of the relevant files: one form into my Daily Prompter, one into the file on my colleague, and one into my file on ideas for publications. No matter where I conceivably look for this paperwork, I'll find it, or I'll find a cross-reference form sending me directly to it.

SAMPLE CROSS-REFERENCE FORM

Item name: How to Organize Your Work and Your Life
Description: book on improving my effectiveness
Location: shelf 1, window bookcase
Cross-reference key words: time management, saving time, white-collar, productivity, goals, my mission, success

3) ACTIVE VS. INACTIVE FILES

I like to keep my project files lean and extremely current, so I clean out any information I haven't worked on in three months or more. I keep these "past projects" files in strict order and readily accessible, but separate from my active files.

The thinnest neglected files I cull are easy to handle: I just pull them from the current file drawer and slip them in with other "past projects" in the next room. But when I finish with a long, drawn-out, complex project that has three to six inches of material in the file, I usually take a few moments to go through it and put the papers in sensible order:

a) I staple all relevant correspondence together, in chronological order, latest on top.
b) I substitute staples for paper clips throughout (to prevent inadvertent couplings among my papers).
c) I remove unwanted duplicates and unused reference materials, notes, or whatever. I retain only what actually contributed to the making of the project.
d) I remove generally useful reference materials, replacing them with cross-reference forms, and file the materials where they should be in my system.

When I'm done, I have a minimal (yet comprehensive) file reflecting the work I put into the project, stacked in sensible order so I can leave it for five years and yet recapture what I did should I look through it again. I am free to forget the details of past projects, knowing I can (and frequently do) refresh my memory whenever I need to.

4) REFERENCE FILES

A fourth part of the paperwork system is dedicated to Reading and Research. Here you can keep all the articles, books, graphs, and items of interest you hate to lose but can't live with underfoot. As with your current files, you organize here according to your own interests. Create a category or subject heading for each project or homogeneous grouping you want to track.

Simply give each subject heading a number: 100, 200, 300, etc. Then number the items you are saving, consecutively within each

subject heading. For example, articles you save under "Automo-
biles" might be numbered 101, 102, 103, etc. Items you save under
"Recipes" might be numbered 201, 202, 203, etc. If you think
you'll have more than a hundred, number your categories as 1000,
2000, 3000, and so forth.

Store the items in consecutive order, but be sure to use a good
storage method for each. For example, put magazine articles in
binders, folders, or closed boxes of some sort; books on book-
shelves; oversize volumes where you have adequate room, and so
on.

Now here's the heart of this system. List each consecutive numbered item in a subject index: a sturdy piece of paper filed by
subject. (Or you can keep your listings in your computer. More
about automation later on.) Include a brief title, source, date, and
synopsis or main point. Note the file number you assigned the
item. Keep the index up to date and properly filed. This is a bit of
a chore when you are first converting a messy-closet type of system
to something a little more ordered. But each new item takes just a
minute to number, index, and file. Even if you leave your present
files strictly alone, make the resolution to file everything new according to this system. The payoffs over the long run will be stag-
gering.

Assuming you have some items filed this way, watch what happens when you want to find one of them:

You're sitting and reflecting on some topic that's important to
you, say, beech trees. Suddenly, the light in your head goes on and
you say to yourself, "Didn't I read something on this just a few
months back? Or was that a few years back?" Armed with your
new filing system, you pull the index sheets (or check your
computer) for "Beech Trees" (or "Trees" or other key words you
think of) and quickly scan the titles, synopses, or sources to refresh
your memory. Yes! You find the item you want, number 379. Your
brief synopsis shows you it's the item you remembered. You put
back the index sheets and go right to where you keep item 379.
In three minutes, you have found an article you haven't seen or
thought about for three years! And you went right to it!

What would you have done without this system? How could
you have found this article? Would you have looked over seventy-
nine articles in the subject heading to find this one item? Time-
consuming and boring. Hardly likely. And would you have recog-

nized it if you had looked? Possibly not. Would you have remembered the critical information about this article well enough to have found it in some library? Would you have taken the time and trouble to do so? Would it have been a worthwhile use of your time if you had? In my experience, most people would take a "sour grapes" attitude and do without the information they wanted.

Notice I'm not proposing you use this Reading and Research file to keep everything that ever crosses your desk that you might conceivably, sometime, possibly, perhaps want to look at again before you retire or die. No, that is not how we select the items we want to retain.

Too many people decide to retain reference material or interesting items on the basis of their answer to the question "Could I possibly want to see this again?" That's the wrong question, because the answer will almost always be "Yes."

A more relevant and useful question is: "If I don't save this information, how hard would it be to find it (or something equivalent) again?" Most of the time, you don't need to save items, because you can replace them relatively easily with the same or newer items from library collections. Sure, it's a little less convenient to go retrieve articles from distant libraries rather than from your own collection. But we're concentrating here on making good use of your time and efforts, and you can usually do more productive things than play librarian with your own materials, particularly when paid librarians are around to keep materials anyway.

Save yourself a lot of filing bother by getting a list of publications received by libraries to which you have easy access. Keep it around and don't save articles from those publications unless they are of extreme relevance and timely value. What you should save, though, are: a) quick-reading items you intend to read, scan, or clip from and then throw away, and b) unusual items you may not find in libraries readily available to you.

Another problem in deciding what to save and what to toss is the gray area of partially valuable material you'd like to save because—now get this—you might not remember it exists when you want information on that topic sometime later. This gray area has been bothering me for years, causing me to clutter my files with junk I never look at because I might want to look at it sometime—and how would I ever even know it exists unless I save it? A perfect example would be those "advertorials" paid for by large corporations explaining various problems, like energy shortages, educational crises, and job layoffs, to the average person. They are not listed in any public index or reference work I know. Yet I might want those on a particular topic for an article or a book five years from now. So I save representative samples. Sheer junk!

The solution: Take notes on the dates the ads appeared, with a brief synopsis of the explanation they offer, and file these notes under the particular topic headings in your general filing system. When you want them, refer to the newspapers in which they appeared, which public libraries are certain to have on file for you. Voilà!

5) PLANS AND DREAMS

The fifth part of your filing system is oriented toward the future. Here you keep track of your short- and long-range plans, your hopes and dreams, your random and/or brilliant ideas—anything you want to preserve for future refinement and possible implementation.

You can save all these items in chronological order by the date you first filed them. If there is just too much to leaf through conveniently, you can also sort them by category, by subject, and by level of refinement as you move the items along from initial conception to final implementation.

6) GENERAL REFERENCE

Another equally important section of your files will be for general reference. Here you can store the names of all those people you met at conferences and cocktail parties, the titles of books you mean to read, scribbled maps of how to get to your friends' houses, and little booklets you get at tourist agencies or government offices. If you want to save something and you can't find a specific place, you can always stick it in here with good hopes of finding it again.

Most of us lose things in alphabetic files as easily as we lose keys in the snow. But you don't have to. Simply get in the habit of filing (and retrieving) items by what they are about rather than by what they are.

For example, say you meet a congressman who promises to help you land a big government contract next time you visit Washington, D.C. Don't file his name alphabetically. You may not remember it when you're ready to leave for the Capitol. Instead, carefully place this name in your file under "Government," "Washington," "Sales," or "Congressman," depending on what mental road you take when you think of this opportunity. To be safe, cross-reference this name under all the possibilities.

Or, say you are trying to file a company booklet that tells you how to save money on your car insurance. Don't file it under "Allstate" or "State Farm," where you'll never look for it. File it under the generic category of "Insurance" or "Car." To be even more ingenious, place the booklet in your Daily Prompter timed to surface again a few weeks before you must renew your current auto insurance policy. Then you will see it again automatically when, and only when, you are likely to want to act on it.

What about the names of local baby-sitters? Under "B." Your family doctor? Under "D." What about that book you want to look for and read? Not under the title—you'll forget it. Leave a note in your file under the book's subject or under "Reading." To be doubly sure you're reminded of the book, put a cross-reference slip in your Daily Prompter a month or so into the future.

7) YOUR TRAVEL FILE

A file on travel information is an important resource worth the trouble to maintain, but only if you travel a lot or enjoy travel very much. Use this part of the system strictly to keep tract of facts, maps, and useful information regarding places you want to (or feel you may) visit.

For example, business travelers (and others) can keep a separate folder for each location they visit regularly, plus other folders for cities, counties, countries, or continents they hope to see someday. Store here all the interesting articles, relevant maps, tips from people who have been there, and (where possible) experiences you garner yourself—anything that may help you en route to or in specific locations.

Bring the appropriate files with you when you travel. Then, when you're sitting in your hotel room, bored silly and desperate for something to do, you can turn off the tube and search your files for a nice restaurant, an exciting theater or show, a colorful district or neighborhood, or whatever interests you. Keep track of your good and bad experiences in each location, too, so you can repeat those you want to and avoid those you don't, without wasting any time or effort the second time through a town.

Creating a Paperwork System

START WITH A WASTEBASKET

One of the best tools for cutting down the size of your paperwork pile is a *large* wastebasket—the best place to put a good portion of the paper that comes your way. But once the wastebasket is full, people often find other—more lasting—places for perfectly good trash. This is a shame, since paperwork you place in the wastebasket will not come back to haunt you, whereas paperwork you store on your desk or in your files will take up a tremendous amount of space and time, no matter how worthless it may be intrinsically.

It's nearly always useful to divide your incoming papers before you tackle them, and a large wastebasket is invaluable as a destination for the least important part of your incoming paper stream. One good paperwork sorting system involves the following categories:

a) Handle Immediately—don't put it down without taking some action on it.

b) Interesting or Useful/Read and Save—your Primary Reading, a good category for valuable materials you really should know about.

c) Interesting or Useful/Read and Discard—your Secondary Reading, a larger category in which to place materials it would be valuable to peruse, but which you may reasonably neglect when you have other demands on your time. If you don't read an item in this group within, say, two weeks, out it goes.

d) File Under Name—here's where you note how to file an item and temporarily collect all your items to be filed until your assistant can take care of them, or (if you work

alone) until you can take the time to do the filing
yourself.
e) File 13—the wastebasket.

DO A PRELIMINARY SORT

If you have someone to help you, let him or her sort your paperwork before you see it, according to this or some other system
that makes sense to you. If you have no help, take a few moments
before you start your paperwork to sort it thoroughly. Here's how:

a) Stack your incoming paperwork on your otherwise clean
   desk or work surface. Let no other papers be present for
   this ceremony. Have your stapler and a bold-colored
   marker ready.
b) Pick up each item in your nonwriting hand, scan it
   quickly, and decide what to do with it, using the five
   categories listed above as your criteria for the next step.
c) File your trash immediately.
d) Mark items to file according to subject and annotate
   with key words to help in cross-referencing each item for
   later retrieval. Write all this boldly at the top, right on
   the front of the papers. If you don't want to mark them,
   staple (clips or adhesives are untrustworthy) notepaper
   to the front and write on that. Make one stack of everything to be filed.

   In this stack include reference material and other records for filing. Put your notes and original paperwork
   earmarked for your Daily Prompter here, too. Basically,
   if the item doesn't require your attention immediately,
   put it here for filing so you can find it later, or so it will
   come up by itself just when you need it later on.
e) Stack up materials you want for Read and Save. Put
   them in a convenient folder, with the newest items on
   top. Take this Primary Reading file with you everywhere, and when you get a few minutes, pull off the top
   item and read it on the spot. Then mark it for filing, or
   toss it away. Read from the top because this sort of material generally doesn't age well. It's more useful to read
   the newer, more relevant material first.

Because this Primary Reading can be so important in trying to accomplish your goals, you owe yourself some reading time built into your schedule.

When your Read and Save folder gets too thick, pull off items from the bottom and quickly reevaluate their worth before you throw them away. They may be out of date, superseded by other reading matter, or irrelevant to your current interests. Scan them. Don't read them to see if they are worth your time, because if you do, you'll be intrigued (you were once before, when you first put this item in the folder, remember?). Or worse, you'll feel so guilty for not reading the item so far ("I really should read this") that you'll stop your really important work to read the thing right now. Retain only what you really want.

f) Stack up materials for your Read and Discard folder—your lower-priority reading. If this file gets too thick, simply pull items from the bottom and toss without looking at them. You haven't had time for these things, and so you certainly don't have the time to see whether you might have time for them in the future. If you do find time to read something from this file, just skim the piece, looking for what's relevant or useful, and toss the paper out of your life.

g) Deal immediately with a piece of paperwork you can't throw away or file. If it's a letter, reply to it right now. If it requires some fact-finding or planning, take the first steps right now. If it requests a decision, make it right now, or start the decision-making process as best you can.

If the paperwork signals a large project, begin by making a step-by-step plan for completing it. Then get started on the first step right now. If you are not ready to go that far, at least start the preparation process by writing the preliminary letters or inquiries, making the initial phone calls, doing the initial thinking, or whatever.

In general, you can make better use of your time simply by

handling the paper in front of you rather than by shuffling it hither and yon a few times before putting your mind in gear to work on it.

There are exceptions, however. If someone sends you a book and asks you to read it, for example, you don't have to finish all 592 pages before you pick up the next paperwork item. But even so, you should put the book where you can find it again, and make a mental or a written plan about when, where, or if you will read it. That done, you can turn to the next item on your desk. At this point, I hope it goes almost without saying: If you make such a plan, you should follow it.

ELIMINATE REPETITION

One source of paperwork drudgery is the curse of endless repetition. For example, information from one report has to be reworked or copied onto one, two, or three other reports. And this goes on every week, sometimes every day. Or you get frequent requests for the answers to the same questions. Or you must make the same statements or initiate the same requests time and time again in the course of whatever you're trying to do.

You can save a lot of this repeat time by taking a few extra minutes to provide some alternatives. For a few dollars you can buy personal labels (gummed or pressure-sensitive) in your favorite stationery store, or even by mail order. Look around, you'll see the offers. Even though you have stationery, personal labels save you half a minute or more every time you give your name and/or address. Such labels are one of the most profitable small investments you can make. If you don't like labels, perhaps you can have a rubber stamp or a paper-embosser made with the information you need to repeat.

For situations where you need to copy information onto a form, start using duplication equipment. Make it a policy never to handwrite the same information twice. With this mindset, you will find many opportunities to save time using mechanical copying. You may save only a few seconds each time, but in the long run you will save hours, even days, of monklike copying by hand.

These days most offices have good copiers, and copy stores inhabit every neighborhood. Make a machine copy and attach it to the new form instead of copying the information by hand. Or make a machine copy and cut-and-paste the information you want to transfer. Not only is this faster, but there's no chance for hand-copying errors that can waste even more of your time when they come back to haunt you. (There's more on eliminating needless duplication in the section on computers.)

Inexpensive printing is another great way to eliminate needless repetition of standard answers to the most commonly asked questions. The next time you answer what seems like a standard or very familiar question, write down your answer and have duplicates run off. File them where you can find them again. Then, next time that standard question comes in, just reach into your files for the answer, staple it to the question (if it comes via correspondence), and send it out.

Try the same procedure for standard questions you ask others or for standard statements you make to others via your paperwork. Get the question or statement printed and you will never have to write or type or dictate the darn thing again.

If you want to get a little more elaborate, combine half a dozen or so of your standard answers on a single sheet of paper. Then simply circle or check off the appropriate one(s) on a copy and send it off. We've all received these forms from government agencies, banks, and other institutions. They don't make a very personal impression, but do save your precious time.

CREATE A "BOOK" OF PARAGRAPHS

For correspondence requiring more than a check mark on a standard form, you can usually save time by creating your own "book" of common paragraphs. Go through your past letters and memos, or start fresh from today. Collect your best paragraphs on all the subjects that frequently appear in your writings. Compile them into a loose-leaf binder (or into your computer), organized by subject or some other appropriate scheme. Give each paragraph a code number. If you have a typist, make sure he or she gets duplicates with the exact same code numbers on the paragraphs.

SAMPLE SELECTION OF PARAGRAPHS

1. Thanks very much for your suggestion on how to improve customer service at the "Will Call" window. Unfortunately, we have tried your suggestion before and we find that people are less satisfied with that approach than with our present system. But we nevertheless appreciate your interest, and hope we can keep serving you in the future.
2. Thanks very much for your suggestion on how to improve customer service at the "Will Call" window. Your idea appears to have a great deal of merit, and we are looking into possibilities for testing it sometime soon. We certainly appreciate your interest, and hope we can keep serving you in the future.
3. Thanks very much for your suggestion on how to improve customer service at the "Will Call" window. Your idea appears to have a great deal of merit, and we will be using it starting next month. We certainly appreciate your interest, and hope we can keep serving you in the future.

With the book of common paragraphs completed, creating correspondence becomes relatively easy. Just leaf through your binder (or computer file) until you find the paragraphs you want to use. Make notes to yourself for each letter you want to write, or specify the paragraphs to your typist by code number. Be sure to list the code numbers in the order you want the paragraphs typed. Now give the name, address, and subject heading (see "Learn Direct Writing Skills," page 79) and you're done. The letter will say just what you want it to, but the work takes only a fraction of the time it would otherwise have taken.

If you don't like your own writing or don't want to make your own book, you can buy books (or computer disks) full of letters on a wide variety of topics. Check your local business library or computer catalog for such books and give them a trial run before you buy.

LET OTHERS DO IT

A basic credo of maximizing your results, applied here to paperwork, is to let other people do as much as possible for you. If you find yourself spending too much time on paperwork of too little importance to your goals, look around for opportunities to let other people do it: employees or subordinates, people who send you the paperwork, people who expect the paperwork from you, and payroll, accounting, clipping, reading, or other specialized service organizations you can pay to do some of your paperwork.

It's easiest if you already have a secretary or assistant. Let him or her take over the chore of sorting your mail. After a week or two of demonstrating how you handle your daily mail call, you can probably delegate most of this time-consuming chore. From then on:

a) You need never see junk mail again unless you want to. (Even then, your secretary can throw the stuff in a box in the closet, where you can dig through it for your own enjoyment when you're not busy with something more important.) This relieves you of a great burden, particularly when you are under pressure to perform.

b) You need never handle routine inquiries again. Your secretary can learn the responses to four out of five of the items people send you. Teach your secretary to give these responses and you automatically free yourself for more important activities. Nor

c) need you compose routine correspondence ever again. With the aid of your collected paragraphs, or with a little native writing skill and some direction from you, almost any secretary can compose the bulk of the letters, memos, reports, and other items required from you. Give up this chore—although you should probably supervise this work until you feel confident it is going well. Incidentally, don't pressure people to handle routine work perfectly. Doing it adequately takes far less time without compromising effectiveness too much.

Even without a secretary, let people who work for you handle the portion of your paperwork that relates to them. For example, one department supervisor in a large manufacturing company had to spend hours every week filling in production reports that detailed how much each worker in his group had turned out during the preceding week. He began saving 80 percent of this time by letting each of these people keep track of his or her output directly on the forms. He merely checked over what the workers wrote. After a few months, he felt confident making only spot verification checks, which saved even more of this paperwork time.

In another situation, a group leader was supposed to read a long-winded article and pass on the relevant portion to his group. He took thirty minutes off his paperwork time simply by making copies of the appropriate paragraphs from the report and distributing them to the right people.

Whatever amount of help you have or don't have, you can handle casual or in-house correspondence more quickly by writing your response directly on the originals sent you. Run a machine copy for your files (when necessary) and send the original right back where it came from.

In addition, you can look for other ways to put more of the burden on the people who send you the paperwork. For example, a bank recently sent me an application form for a loan. I sent it right back clipped to a copy of another bank's loan application that had all the pertinent information. I included a signed, handwritten note that said, "Here is all the information I believe you need. Let me know if you need anything further." My idea was to let them neatly copy the details into those tiny blank spaces. I had more important things to do.

KEEP RELEVANT PAPERWORK TOGETHER

Sometimes you spend more time filing and retrieving relevant papers you work on than you actually spend doing the work. If this happens to you, stop putting that paper back in the file. Keep the entire bundle clipped securely into a folder, and let it circulate— but not on your desk—until the project is complete.

For example, you're working to develop a proposal to supply a large customer with widgets at a fair, but low price. To quote prices discounted from the standard price list, you must gather information on manufacturing costs, alternative materials, savings from quantity purchases of raw materials, and other factors. You finally prepare the proposal and send it to your boss for approval. But you save your supporting paperwork, and either attach it to the proposal you send for approval or keep it with the file copy in your office. It may be weeks later that your boss suggests you cut prices another 10 percent, or demands to know how you can dare propose to cut prices as deeply as you have. But you're prepared, because you can immediately pull out the supporting paperwork and quickly find the information you need to refresh your memory of the facts and to revamp the proposal to meet the new requirements.

Of course, this method may not help you much when there are reams of printed materials to consult, large circulation lists, classified data you cannot let out of your office, or projects you complete by working in long stretches with only short interruptions or delays. But if you look for chances, you'll find plenty of opportunities to use this technique.

Tips for an Effective Office System

ARRANGE PHYSICAL SPACE

Paperwork is a physical process, so don't overlook the need for adequate physical facilities to handle the paper flow. For example, if you look at blueprints or large layouts, you need a large expanse of work space on which you lay them flat. You need adequate lighting. And you probably need efficient storage for other large papers you keep around. Without adequate equipment, you're wasting your time.

If you receive large volumes of paperwork each day, you need the physical facilities to store it, process it, and pass it along or file it. Take a few moments right now to trace the flow of paper around you. Check at each "way station" to verify there is enough room for your normal flow of paper; enough supplies; enough work space; and enough storage for incoming and outgoing paper so you don't have to live with piles of it all around you.

Once you have everything off your desk, and neatly filed somewhere in your Comprehensive Filing System, you can turn your attention to the physical placement of all these papers. There's almost certainly not enough room to have all this material—whether in filing cabinets or old shoe boxes—within arm's reach.

So separate your materials according to how frequently you turn to them. Try to arrange your paperwork and materials roughly in concentric circles. What you need most frequently should be within arm's reach. The next group should be within a step or two. The next group within several steps, and so on right out the door. This way, you'll automatically save time and energy in the ordinary course of accomplishing what you want.

Files, reference materials, and current-project folders you use several times a day belong within easy reach—although not directly on your desk. A low table, cabinet, or set of shelves behind or alongside your work space can hold these items out of sight, but ready when you need them.

You can place other files, project files, and reference materials you use less frequently across the room from where you normally work. Dead storage and items you look at only once or twice a year do not deserve to be in your workroom at all. Keep them out in the hall, in an adjacent room, in a locked storage room, or elsewhere.

UTILIZE TIME LIMITS

Self-imposed time limits are an excellent tool for reorganizing the goals you work toward.

Essentially, you should create a self-imposed time limit—a maximum daily or weekly allocation of effort—to a specific project or type of work. For example, you might decide to limit your paperwork to five hours per week. This means you'll keep careful track of the time you spend on paperwork, and when you finish your fifth hour of the week, you stop. That's it! No more! Any leftover paperwork will have to wait until next week to receive your attention, someone else will have to do it, or it will have to find a place in some other category in your time schedule.

One shop manager I know began limiting his paperwork to seven hours per week. One week he reached his time limit before he had had a chance to review his inventories and order more raw materials. On Thursday, some of his unfinished paperwork came back to him as an emergency shortage of raw materials. So he handled it then.

You can be a little smarter in setting your limits by evaluating your work load and giving yourself enough time to do your important tasks—just enough! You reduce the value of your time limits if they give you enough room to include irrelevant or worthless activities.

Refer to a current Time Log to see how much time you are spending on your paperwork. (The Time Log, explained in detail in Appendix A, is the most accurate method of self-measuring how much time you spend on various activities throughout your work day, week, month, and year. Since you note the activities with which you fill each time interval throughout the day, your Time Log provides an incontrovertible document that details your actual time-use patterns.)

Is your paperwork really worth as much of your time as you give it? If you haven't yet done very much to let other people help you, to avoid senseless redundancies, to clear your desk, and to sort before you work, you can probably set your paperwork time limit to half of what you currently spend on it. If this seems too drastic, try reducing your time spent on paperwork by 10 percent a month for a few months. You'll be surprised how much you can cut. Almost everyone I have worked with has safely reduced his or her paperwork time by 40 to 60 percent with no loss in final effectiveness.

How to Handle Special Correspondence

Special correspondence is more than routine paperwork: It's the unique letter, the original proposal, the personal reply, the expert analysis, the communication that can come only from you. You would have a hard time trying to standardize this material, and most likely it would not be very desirable for you to do so. But that doesn't mean you have to waste time or lower your overall effectiveness level when turning out special correspondence.

The key is to be as thoughtful and original in deciding how to get your special message across as you are in creating your message. For example:

CALL, DON'T WRITE

Sometimes, you can get the message across very quickly and effectively with a phone call rather than a letter. For example, when

I was publishing a newsletter, I regularly received dozens of letters from writers wanting assignments. I hardly ever took action on any of them. But I will always remember the impression one writer made on me with a phone call. I experienced her enthusiasm directly, and I found myself giving her extra points for having taken the initiative to call me. I gave her an assignment on the spot, whereas letter writers had to wait. The phone call worked out well for both of us, saving our time and reducing the demand for laborious correspondence, as well as serving to increase her effectiveness in getting what she wanted.

But in other cases, there may be a smaller or a less obvious time saving. For example, it may be possible to make an initial contact by telephone, or even to conduct detailed discussions or negotiations. But it's usually impossible to close a sale or conclude a final agreement without some sort of follow-up correspondence.

Evaluate each of your special messages, then decide whether the telephone or the typewriter will be more effective. The phone may be faster—even cheaper if you include the cost of your time. But you may not save as much if the message requires a letter anyway. A letter may be the better medium for your message if you want more time to think out and polish your remarks. You can rewrite what you say until you get it right. However, on paper you lose both the give-and-take and the emotional contact you can sometimes achieve via direct electronic connection.

LET YOUR SECRETARY WRITE IT

By definition, you must be the one to originate most, if not all, of the special correspondence you send out. But this does not imply you must be the one to physically produce it.

For example, letters going out over your signature are yours, even though you may not type them. Similarly, correspondence pulled together under your direction is yours, even though you may not be the writer. Clearly, you can free a lot of your time from special correspondence and devote yourself to other work by letting others handle this writing. Just be sure you are satisfied with the results.

To make this work, you must initially devote some time toward training the person who will do your special writing for you. How much time this takes depends partly on his or her ability to write and partly on your skills as a trainer. Slowly introduce your assistant to the job by letting him or her write a few of your special correspondence items with you. Incorporate his or her ideas, where appropriate, but stick with your wordings and pet phrases as much as possible. As you gain confidence in your surrogate's writing ability, let him or her handle more of your writing chores. For a while, check everything before it is sent out. In the next stage, let him or her write more of your correspondence, then you check it briefly just before signing it. Finally, when you become totally comfortable with his or her judgment and work, you can give all your special correspondence to your surrogate and perhaps join the ranks of those who no longer sign or even see their own letters!

HANDWRITTEN REPLIES SAVE TIME

Check out your letter-writing process—from your initial desire to write, through first and second drafts, rough typing, rewriting, and retyping, all the way out the door. Is what you must say in your replies always worth all this? If not (and who can truthfully answer "Yes"?), try a quick solution: handwrite your brief letters and notes and immediately send them off.

Sure, they may not look as pretty as formal typewritten letters. But in most cases they will get your message across satisfactorily in a fraction of the time typewritten letters require. And they can lend a desirable personal touch to an otherwise austere and cold communication.

To facilitate this option, use half-sheet notepaper (5½ by 8½ inches)—imprinted or plain. Write neatly, and sign legibly. Then make a file copy and send off the original. This may save you only a few minutes in each instance, but over the many instances your time and personal energy savings will mount up.

MAKE IT 90 PERCENT PERFECT

This trick is guaranteed to make some of you angry, even outraged—or at least upset. The idea is simply to reduce your standards for selected special correspondence from 100 percent to 90 percent perfect. The time savings are well worth the compromise.

Notice I'm saying "selected" correspondence. If you are writing a proposal for a million-dollar contract, you might decide to check every comma and question mark, intent on making it absolutely perfect. If it's 1787 and you are making a handwritten copy of the Constitution, to be signed by the Continental Congress—again, you might want to start over a few times until you get it letter-perfect. Thomas Jefferson certainly did.

But how many of those items do you write in a day? Most people pore over their precious prose as though it were timeless verse, yet it usually gets no farther than the local bulletin board, the desk of someone just as overburdened as you, or your mother's house. Except for your mother, does anyone care if you've mistyped "the" as "teh" and fixed it with a neat ballpoint pen? Believe me: No one will disparage you for a few timely xxxxxx's.

You may not believe my words, but take courage and try this technique. Allow an imperfection in your correspondence, once or twice and see if anyone notices or cares. Chances are, no one will. You'll cut time off your special correspondence in this way with little or no reaction from your readers.

LEARN DIRECT WRITING SKILLS

Direct writing is the art of saying what you mean, as accurately as possible, in a relatively short time and space. Unlike the formal business correspondence style you learned in school, the direct writing format can exclude the formal salutation (in favor of the subject line), paragraph indentations, and flowery opening and closing paragraphs. It features, when appropriate, a numbered listing of items rather than a narrative flow of words. All of this cuts some typing time, as well as time required to compose what's being typed.

A subject line instead of the standard "Dear—" salutation states very succinctly what the communication is about. For example:

SUBJECT: NOTES ON OUR RECENT MEETING
or
SUBJECT: YOUR REQUEST FOR LEAVE IN SOMALILAND

Once you get past the shock of seeing such direct communication in a letter, you begin to realize how beneficial a well-focused subject line can be. It not only sets the mood for the entire letter, it saves you whole sentences right away.

Instead of:

Dear John:
I have been thinking very hard about your request for leave time in
Somaliland, and want to let you know what I am thinking. I don't
believe this is the appropriate time to approve such a request.

you can say:

RE: YOUR REQUEST FOR LEAVE IN SOMALILAND
I don't think this is the appropriate time to approve such a request.

The art of direct writing is harder than it looks. Your first step
must be to develop your interest in doing it, after which you will
quickly learn to edit and condense your ideas before you write.
Then, simply practice every chance you get and you will gradually
and continuously improve.

IMPROVING YOUR READING AND WRITING

It's almost unbelievable, but the four popular ways people take
in and give out information have remained virtually unchanged for
a thousand years. We still do our reading, writing, speaking, and
listening almost exactly the way our ancestors did. And yet, consider how much more information we try to take in and give out
in a lifetime.

We'll tackle the skills you need for effective speaking and listening when we discuss meetings. Here we can concentrate on
better use of your time when reading and writing.

Speed Reading

It goes almost without saying that one basic way to improve
your use of reading time is simply to read faster. Programs to teach
you speed-reading skills are widely available through community
colleges, local learning centers, and private schools or training programs. There are also very effective books and training tapes. To
my knowledge, they all teach the same speed-reading skills.

I suggest you learn these skills and use them where appropriate.
It just doesn't make sense to read at 200 words per minute when

you can gather the same information at 300, 400, or 500 words per minute. You do enough reading that even a 10 percent boost in reading speed will free up significant hours for other items on your agenda.

Skimming and Scanning

The bane of most slow readers is their overwhelming desire to read every single word, usually in order. This will kill your reading speed. To understand why, imagine a situation in which your TV tuner is locked. You must watch an entire day's programming on a single channel before you can switch one channel in either direction. It could take you a solid week just to move to the station you want! This would certainly discourage channel changing, and no doubt limit your enjoyment. Fortunately, you are perfectly free to change channels any time you like, as often as you like, as many channels in either direction as you like. Doesn't that give you a great deal of freedom to pick and choose the best of what is broadcast?

If you choose to exercise it, you have the same freedom with printed materials: the freedom to start on any page, read as much or as little as you like, and skip as far as you like in either direction as often as you like. So why limit yourself to plodding from start to finish, word by word, page by page? When you break free of these limitations, you start skimming and scanning.

We can define skimming as the act of running your eyes quickly over a printed page, picking out headings, charts, and other eye-catching items. In skimming, you try to catch the main points on a printed page by reading only the prominent details. You can look at first and last sentences of paragraphs, too, since they usually offer good clues to the main points under discussion.

Scanning, on the other hand, is the careful examination of the outline or construction of a piece of writing, with a view toward understanding it without reading it. In scanning, you look at the table of contents, the list of illustrations, charts and/or tables, the index, and the appendices. You try to determine what the writing is about, and you try to zero in on the location of the most important ideas. Only when you think you have located them do you turn to those pages and begin to skim.

To save time, you do a minimum of word-by-word reading, mainly when you have trouble understanding the meaty parts on your first or second skim. In traditionally structured research articles and business reports, for example, you may read only the summary. In other texts, you may do no reading at all, or you may read only the few paragraphs you have identified as being most important to you. This breakaway from word-by-word reading doesn't occur overnight. It may take you a while to break old habits, or to get comfortable reading so few words per page. Nevertheless, skimming and scanning are valuable means to cover more ground in a given reading time.

Collected Readings

Concentration is a basic principle for getting better results. Just as the assembly line helps people turn out larger numbers of similar items, concentrating or bunching similar tasks gives you assembly-line advantages. You can apply this to your reading by collecting materials you intend to read and sitting down to read them all at once. You can do even better by grouping materials on a single subject or a small set of related topics.

Your Read and Save/Read and Discard files serve as good places to collect important material. Or you can create a set of special subject files in which you collect what you want to read for your next scheduled reading session.

The Reading Hour

Armed with a collection of similar items to read, and dedicated to your skimming-and-scanning tactics, your next step is to sit down and read. But here, too, you can get more done in less time with a subtle shift in old habits.

Bunch your reading time! That's the secret. Sure, you can make five ordinarily wasted minutes a little more fruitful by reading something from one of your reading files. But that's not the way to get your reading done. Instead, dedicate one hour per week, or more, to pure and simple reading.

Find a comfortable location and secure yourself against interruptions for at least an hour. That's a good time period for deep concentration without fatigue. If you need more reading time and you can go longer at a stretch, do so. If you need less reading time, do the one-hour session less often. For the hour, sit comfortably with a decent light on your reading, and scan, then skim each piece. Make notes about relevant information right on the paper (unless it's a book you cannot mark up, in which case make separate notes keyed to the book's page numbers).

Some people work through their reading faster if they use a timer to limit their attention on a single item to ten minutes or less (time limits again). But this depends on your personal style. It doesn't matter how you do it, so long as you work through each reading item quickly and accurately. Your notes save you time later by speeding recall of what you have read without requiring you to rescan and reskim the item.

Cooperative Reading

Some people have a great deal of must-do reading: for their jobs, their hobbies, or personal interests and enjoyment. But they have too many other commitments to allow enough time for reading.

The solution can be a cooperative reading setup. In this technique, you share your reading load with others who have the same or similar reading needs. For example, an engineering group at an aerospace company has more required reading to keep current in the field than its members can possibly handle on their own. So they have formed a six-headed reading cooperative. Each member reads only one-sixth of the journals and articles he or she would have to read individually. Twice a month the group holds a briefing where each member reports on the good items he or she has found, and gives reference information so anyone interested can find and read the original piece.

The Summary Statement

When it comes to reading and writing, one of the best ways to save everyone's time is to give and demand a summary statement. This is a short paragraph that summarizes the subject, facts, and conclusions of the material to be read.

For best results, put the summary statement at the very beginning of the piece. In a lengthy report, you might place it on its own page. For a shorter report, just set it off by separate margins on the first page.

A summary statement saves the reader's time by providing the gist of the piece in a few seconds of reading. Then it's up to the reader to decide whether or not to continue. The writer benefits, too, from the summary statement. Not only will more people read the piece, but they will probably read it sooner because the summary statement gives most people what they want quickly. If you're waiting for an answer to what you've written, your summary statement will facilitate both reading and responding to your piece. In fact, in some cases you can write a good enough summary statement and leave off the main body of text. No one will miss it, and you'll save time in the writing.

Time to Cook Before Composing

The secret ingredient for better and faster writing is to take the time to *study* the material you're going to write about, to be sure you understand it thoroughly. Then outline what you want to say, or at least determine what you want to achieve with your writing.

Now comes the cooking part: Put the work aside for a day or more. Let your subconscious mind (some would say the right half of your brain) ponder the problem and live with it. If you have enough time, don't rush into any writing. Wait for inspiration to strike you. Sure, writing is 10 percent inspiration and 90 percent perspiration, but you might as well have that 10 percent extra if you can get it. Even if you cannot wait for full inspiration, the time you give yourself to "simmer" the material will result in a better blended, more effective piece of writing.

Dictate, Don't Handwrite

If you're moving through this book in traditional fashion—word by word—you may have come across a section advising you to handwrite some or all of your correspondence. And now I'm telling you the opposite! Well, read a little further and you'll see I'm talking about two different kinds of writing.

In general, if it takes more than five or ten minutes to write it, don't write it at all: dictate.

Dictating has at least three important advantages over writing by hand:

a) You can talk two or three times faster than you can write by hand; sometimes, this multiple climbs as high as five or six. There's a clear time-saving advantage here, despite the stop/start nature of most dictation.
b) You can dictate comfortably in situations where writing is impossible. For example, you can dictate while driving, while riding in jostling trains, while walking, even while lying in bed with the lights out.
c) Few of us feel comfortable dictating unless we have a very good idea of the points we're trying to make. Almost anyone can write pure emptiness without a moment's preparation, and some can even make it sound good. Because dictating is so difficult if you are unprepared, sticking with dictation may drive you to prepare more fully and thus to produce better material than you would by writing off the top of your head.

If you have a secretary, it's doubly advantageous to dictate to a machine rather than a person. This way, your secretary can stay busy while you get the material on tape, cutting required "people hours" by one-third. Also, tests have shown transcription typing to be faster than typing from shorthand notes.

To make your dictation go smoothly, it's advisable to make some written notes prior to speaking your first word. Depending on your dictation skill, you will want anything from a total outline to a simple list of words to jog your memory. Whatever you have in front of you, follow it. Don't let the machine set your pace; make sure it serves you. Also, you might find it helpful to:

a) Practice dictation a few times before trying it for real
b) Cross off items on your outline as you cover them, to prevent repetition
c) Review the whole dictated piece before sending it for transcription.

It's most important, though, to think of your dictated material as a first draft only. This way, you won't be so nervous or difficult to please. You'll still save time by dictating a first draft, then making corrections in pencil—especially when compared with the time cost of handwriting the first draft yourself and then having someone decipher your handwriting. Don't forget: As you gain dictating skill, your first-draft material will get closer and closer to final-draft quality.

You'll find more dictation tips in Chapter 8.

Working with Professional Writers

Corporate presidents and political candidates have long used professionals to write speeches for them. Remember, you can achieve more if you steadily devote your efforts to what you do best, as well as what only you can do. You may be able to claim legitimately that the writing demanded of you is best done by others.

Professional writers require a certain amount of your time in order to give you exactly what you want. But if you have a lot of writing to do, even the time you spend selecting and working with writers will give you an advantage over writing on your own.

GETTING CONTROL OF YOUR TELEPHONE

The telephone may be the greatest time-saving invention developed in modern times. But that doesn't make it perfect. The same telephone that saves you hours of traveling around your city practically every day of your life also interrupts your bath, disturbs your evening meal, makes it easier than ever to waste time in idle conversation, and inevitably gives you a busy signal or keeps you on hold when you are in a hurry.

Get Right to the Point

Telephone conversations are strange combinations of one-to-one meetings and personal letters. You almost always have the urge to be friendly and conversational on the phone, even during business-related talks. Resist! You can save 10 to 30 percent of time spent on the telephone if you carefully limit your conversations to the purpose of your phone calls. Follow these guidelines to keep conversations short, sweet, and to the point:

a) Know what you want to say before you dial. Make a list of key words or main points and check them off as you cover each one. This telephone outline is great for helping you get to the point and stay on it, and for eliminating unnecessary callbacks to clear up the one or two points you missed in your original phone call: The scheduling ideas in Appendix B offer a similar opportunity to outline your calls in advance.

b) Refuse to tie up the other person. Try to cover the purpose of your phone call at once. When that's done you can socialize, if appropriate. But make clear you're ready to hang up the moment the other party wants to.

c) Protect yourself. Insist on knowing the reason the other person called you. Try to take care of this reason quickly and effectively. Then socialize if you want to. But remember you have the right—and the responsibility—to end the conversation the moment you feel pressed by other things you need to do.

Cut Off Overextended Conversations

A long-winded conversation costs you time and results. To cut these costs, take firm action to end the conversation quickly.

The key to success here is perseverance and, when pushed to the limit, your insistence on a quick end to the conversation. Bear in mind that no one can keep you on the telephone if you steadfastly refuse to permit it. You can hold firm, too, provided you have: a) strong motivation, or b) raw courage. Increase your motivation by remembering your important goals and the limits on your opportunities to achieve them. If you feel short on raw courage, I hope this book has been able to help you develop a keen awareness of your goals and how to achieve them. Once you steel yourself to the necessity of cutting off unwanted conversations, you'll benefit from some techniques to make the job a little easier. Here are four:

a) Find a hook. This is the most subtle of the techniques. To work it, you probe gently at the beginning of every conversation for the "hook": a clue to what the other party was doing just prior to the phone call. For example:

CALLER: Hi, Jim.
YOU: Hello, Joe. Say, I thought you always went to lunch at this time of day.
CALLER: No. As a matter of fact, I was just balancing my checkbook when I thought of you.

"Balancing my checkbook" is the hook. Write it down or remember it for later, when you may need it to cut off the conversation. When you're ready to hang up, use the hook like this:

YOU: Well, all right, Joe. I'll let you get back to balancing your checkbook now. Thanks for calling. Bye.

Most of the time, the hook starts the other person thinking about what his or her next task should be. Your hook becomes a natural transition that eases them into hanging up quickly, without making them aware of the power of this technique.

b) Set a timer. You can set a real timer or a mental one. Either way, you say at your first opportunity, "Listen, I have some things to do. I'll have to hang up in about five more minutes." This will often end the conversation on the spot. But when it doesn't, you merely wait a decent interval and say firmly, "Sorry, Joe, but I've got to go now." If you wish, you can add an optional bonus: "I'll talk to you again (soon, later, tomorrow at 3 P.M., next year, etc.)."

This technique is straightforward and honest. I like it. But to use it convincingly, you must truly believe you have something more important to work on. That should be no problem for someone who has come as far through this book as you have!

c) Do them a favor. This is a reversal technique. Once you're ready to cut off the conversation, you say, "Gee, Joe, I know you must be busy. I can't take any more of your time. Bye."

Sometimes Joe will protest by saying, "Oh, no problem, Jim. I've got nothing to do for the rest of the day."

But you keep on with your tactic: "That's nice of you to say, Joe, but I just can't take any more of your time. Bye."

This technique may not work on the first try with everyone, but if you persevere, you'll turn the conversation onto a short track that dead-ends fairly quickly.

d) Make up an excuse. This is the most common tactic. For example:

CALLER: . . . so as I was saying . . .
YOU: Uh-oh. There's someone at the door. I'll have to hang up now. Bye.

Actually, I don't like the dishonesty of this approach, but it does work and many people rely on it. You may as well have it in your arsenal of conversation-ending techniques.

Have a Private Number

This is a valuable technique for making better use of the telephone. The private number excludes most people trying to contact you. They can call on your listed number. But since you know that all the really important calls will come in on your private line, you can screen calls on your listed phone, divert them to an answering machine, or allow the phone to keep ringing indefinitely. Your private number is an emergency hotline people "in the know" can use to reach you no matter how busy you are, no matter what the time or circumstances.

Establish a Telephone Hour

This is a designated part of the day or week in which you use the telephone in a concentrated burst. Your telephone hour is perfect for returning all your phone messages, making your important calls, tracking down information or information sources via the telephone, and keeping in touch with other people on a regular basis. To establish your own telephone hour:

a) Set up a comfortable telephone work space. Furnish it with a good chair, a telephone table, writing tablets and pencils, a calendar, a clock, an alarm or timer system for reminders, and—of course—a telephone.

b) Use your telephone work space for the bulk of your calling. When your hand reaches for the phone at other times, other places, think twice. Try not to call, but instead make a note about whom you wanted to call and the reason.

c) Find a good time of day for your telephone hour. Most people are available during the first two hours of the morning and the last two hours of the evening. Some people are more available during the middle of the day. If you get too many "no answers" or "will call you back" messages during several weeks of your telephone hour, reschedule it for another time of day.

d) Save up your phone messages and return them all during your telephone hour.

e) Keep notes on the calls you make, what both you and the other parties say, and so forth. If you promise someone you'll call back in fifteen minutes, use the timer or alarm to remind you.

f) Obtain the best equipment. Automatic telephone dialers store phone numbers and dial at the touch of a button. They are great. Push-button phones are faster than rotary dialers. Portable phones let you wander and do routine filing or sweeping while you wait on hold or even while you talk. Headsets let you write or type, shuffle papers, or work a calculator while you talk. A few dollars for the right equipment will give you more time and energy for accomplishing your most important goals on the telephone.

Confirm Appointments

You can save yourself a lot of unnecessary travel time if you consistently use the telephone to confirm every appointment just before you start heading for it. Ninety percent of the time, the appointment with your doctor, dentist, colleague, friend, or employer will be "on" as scheduled. Some people you call will even be surprised you had any doubt. But in my experience, often enough to pay big-time dividends, I have found that my appointment was: a) forgotten, b) canceled "just a second ago," or c) "canceled, but we forgot to let you know."

To make this confirmation habit easier, do the following:

a) Whenever you make an appointment to which you must travel, write down the telephone number right next to your reminder of the appointment's date, time, and location.

b) Reserve a few minutes before you leave for your appointment(s) to confirm via telephone.

c) As you confirm each appointment, ask: 1) travel directions (if you have any doubts), and 2) parking directions (if you are going by car). This will save you additional time, as well as concern or worry when you arrive.

d) Use this confirmation call to remind the other person that you'll present yourself as scheduled, and that you'll anticipate his or her being on time, too. You needn't be gruff or pushy about this. It's as easy as saying, "I have another appointment at two-thirty. Do you think Mr. Jones will be available when I get there for our appointment at one o'clock?" With practice, you can learn to

pave your way by telephone and thus minimize the time
you spend in waiting rooms or in fruitless travel.

AUTOMATING TO ORGANIZE
YOUR WORK AND YOUR LIFE

There are several fundamental ways you can use computers to
improve your organization and effectiveness: special-purpose applications, general-purpose applications, and imaginative uses of
either one.

A special-purpose program (or "application") is software that
gives the computer specific capabilities. If you do a specialized
job and there's an application made for that job (hundreds are
commercially available), you can probably increase your effectiveness and productivity by learning to use that application.

Such special-purpose applications include medical office management, flowcharting and project management, special-purpose accounting packages for particular businesses or industries, and
many, many more well-made software packages.

In contrast, a general-purpose application is one that can be
applied to many different situations. The most popular general-
purpose applications include word processing, electronic spreadsheets, computerized accounting systems, database managers, communications programs, business graphics programs, and a few
others. Each gives the computer certain capabilities, leaving it to
the computer user to apply the software to his or her particular
industry, job, or activity. As a practical matter, each of these general-purpose programs can provide a credible substitute for many
of the special-purpose applications.

Of course, the computer opportunities are limited to some degree by present-day constraints on technology, as well as by what
you (or your company) can afford. But these opportunities are
rapidly expanding. The most powerful constraint on computer-
enhanced productivity has always been the individual's limits on
imagination. So let go and think of what a computer ought to do
for you. And never forget the simple rule of computers: "Garbage
in, garbage out." Computerizing a sloppy paperwork system just
gives you a faster sloppy system. Before you computerize, consider
your objectives, then plan what you want to accomplish not only

with the computer but with your work and your life. Don't expect the computer to cure poor planning, foggy goals, or lack of a personal mission. The computer is a tool to help you achieve your goals, but by itself it cannot supply you with goals.

Just as superhighways attract automobile traffic, computing power attracts data processing applications. With computers as inexpensive as they are (too low to advertise, as the retailers say), and with powerful software that lets a computer do more than one thing at a time, it makes great sense for you to take advantage of computer power. Once you start using a computer to help organize your work and your life, you'll steadily find more and more ways to use it.

If you apply just a small portion of the ideas and techniques in this section, you'll benefit greatly from putting a computer in your life.

Computers Never Forget

Assuming no mechanical problems, a computer is the best memory you'll ever have. Once you computerize your calendar, for example, it will reliably remind you of your appointments. Once you enter a name and address, you'll have access to it any time you want—practically forever. If you type into your computer a note on a meeting, you'll be able to review that information on screen or on paper whenever you need to. And once you get a name or any other information entered correctly, it will stay correct and will print out correctly no matter how long you delay or how many times you try it.

But while the computer is near perfect in retaining information, it doesn't require anything more than human approximations from you. After you type (or scan) your notes into a word processor or outlining program, for example, you can call for an immediate electronic search on any fragment you remember—all or part of a name, a date, a subject. In a few seconds, your computer will be ready to display all the tidbits of information that fit the description you provided, and to let you select the right one(s).

What's more, computers remember more than raw facts. They can often be set up to remember what to do with those facts.

Computers Can Repeat Procedures

Let's say you've got a list of customers and a letter asking them to buy more of this week's specially priced product. Once you type the letter and set up the proper commands within your word processing software, your computer will automatically type a separate copy of that letter for every name on your mailing list. Of course, this is a tremendous time saver and productivity improver. But you can go one step further: You can save those word processing commands and use them again as samples, so it will be far easier to have the computer type additional letters to those customers next week, and the week after that! Once you've typed in a list of 100 customers, for example, it's also simple to copy and break down that list into smaller, more specialized mailing lists.

In short, computers can capture not only data but the procedures for making use of data. Thus, everything you do with your computer can be retained and later used as the foundation for doing it again, or doing something similar in a different way.

Many programs have a literal "learn" feature. You turn it on, perform a certain function—perhaps logging onto a financial news system and capturing the closing prices of ten stocks you own or would like to own—and then "save" the commands the computer has "learned." Next time, you can order the computer to execute all those steps on its own.

Because a computer can capture work and do it for you while you do something else, it's a terrific time-saving tool. Once you have a letter, report, graphic, or other item captured, you can reproduce it again effortlessly. This gives you more time and energy with which to make your letters or reports more effective, and more generally useful.

Computers Provide Raw Processing Power

Plenty of cheap computer power makes it possible to complete long, difficult tasks you probably wouldn't attempt with paper-and-pencil calculations or hand-held calculators. Such tasks as mailing-list management, statistical analysis, and keeping track of rapidly changing information on thousands of clients or customers would be onerous to do by hand. But a computer can take care of these and other tasks with ease and efficiency. Here are some ideas on basic computer functions you can use to organize your work and your life.

Use Word Processing for Virtually Any Job

One of the most useful computer programs is the *word processor.* To understand word processing, visualize a typewriter with an endless roll of typing paper. Now visualize picking up individually typed words or letters from the paper and pasting them back down anywhere else on the roll. Also visualize that you can—when you wish—pick up a copy of words or letters and yet leave the original. Finally, visualize that every time you finish moving or copying words, the words automatically rearrange themselves into full lines and pages of text. Now visualize the words automatically spelling themselves correctly (within limits); the page numbers and running heads automatically being added; and perhaps type faces or type sizes changing according to your smallest wishes.

That's word processing.

Notice that word processing has nothing to do with thinking of what to type or how best to say something. Word processing is simply a computerized tool that makes the physical job of typing and later editing your written material as easy as possible. For example, in writing this book, I wrote the sections that follow (on database management and electronic spreadsheets) before I wrote this paragraph. As I started the next section, I realized my thoughts were out of place, so I moved this whole paragraph to this present position with a few simple keystrokes.

The basic advantage of word processing is to simplify your work when you create drafts of letters, memos, reports, fliers, and other printed materials. You can write and save, and later revise earlier versions of these materials without retyping the good parts. You can also print one or one hundred copies of the final material quickly, easily, and inexpensively on a standard computer printer.

What's more, once you have a completed draft stored in a word processor, that text automatically becomes "boiler plate" material you can use in a later writing assignment. In less than a minute, you can call up any combination of your past introductions, conclusions, explanations, definitions, or other word-processed ideas and then insert them into a new letter, memo, or report with minor modifications—or perhaps no modifications at all.

That's benefit enough for most people. But because word processing allows you to print any part of your material, and to have the computer search for a specific combination of letters or words, you can use your computerized word processor for storing and retrieving information, too.

For example, you can maintain a word processing file that contains nothing but a "contact" list of names and addresses. If you need a person's telephone number, you can let the computer search for that name, then read the number right from the screen. When you need a typed envelope, you simply find the right name and address and print those few lines on a label or on the envelope itself. A friend of mine keeps a list of all his wines in the word processor. As he drinks a bottle, or buys new ones, he makes pencil notations on a printed copy of the list. Once a month, he enters all the penciled changes into the electronic version, then prints a fresh copy.

You can type all your appointments, schedules, and laundry or "to do" lists into your word processor, then erase each item as you complete it. If you wish, print the list so you can take it with you away from your desk. Keep copies of the old lists so you can refer to old tasks or re-create proven lists the second and subsequent time you tackle a specific project.

If you can type quickly enough, you can also use the word processor for taking notes on telephone conversations or meetings.

Do Database Management on Your Key Information

A database manager is another among the most useful general-purpose computer programs. A database is simply a collection of information—your personal phone book or Rolodex, your past correspondence, your index card file, payroll or personnel information, and so forth. Once processed mainly by hand, this type of information has found its way into computers more and more often during the past several decades—even in the tiniest businesses. Why? Because the database manager provides the tools for entering, manipulating, and retrieving that information in the wink of an eye, making it significantly more available, more easily utilized, and less expensively manipulated than data kept on paper. The database manager is far more powerful for this kind of work than even a word processor.

One reason is that the data are better organized. Each name, for example, goes into an electronic pigeonhole for names, each street address into a different electronic pigeonhole. In fact, you can and should define separate pigeonholes for each data element. To store a company's or person's contact information, for example, you might have different electronic pigeonholes for each of the following: company name, person's first name, person's last name, street, city, state, zip code, area code, phone number, and fax number. You might even have more.

The database program allows you to search for, sort, and retrieve any or all of the information based on the contents of any of the pigeonholes. For example, you can quickly find everyone with a certain zip code, a certain area code, or a certain last name. The potential time-saving and organizing advantages that flow from this capability are tremendous. Whole books have been written about it, so I won't detail it here. But you'll get an idea of the benefits if you think about using computer power every time you look for specific information. Here are a few examples:

ADDRESS BOOK

Whether you limit your file to frequently called numbers, or you put into your computer just about every name, address, and phone number that crosses your desk, the power of the computer to scan, retrieve, and even print this information can save you hours of work and let you accomplish tasks you might otherwise never attempt.

For example, instead of leafing through the cards of a Rolodex to find a particular person, you can have the computer scan for any portion of the name, address, or other information you typed into the database file. In a few seconds, it's there on the screen so you can dial the number, print an envelope or mailing label, or make other use of the information.

APPOINTMENTS

A list of appointments in your database, sorted by date and time, functions as a simple calendar that never runs out of room. It is also very flexible. For example, if someone postpones an appointment with you, a few keystrokes move the existing notation to its new place in your schedule. If you're leaving your desk or leaving town for a few days, you can easily print a list of all your appointments. You can print two copies, in fact, and use one for crossing off completed assignments, the other for taking notes on what transpired at each meeting.

If you save all your old appointments in a separate file, you're automatically building a great list of personal contacts. Refer to this file to help you recall the right people to approach for each new idea or project you decide to pursue.

FINANCIAL TRANSACTIONS

Each check or charge you sign, each cash expenditure, each bit of income you receive is a financial transaction that has some impact on your budget, your taxes, and your financial well-being. Each investment, each dividend or interest check, each sale of stocks or bonds is also a financial transaction. And you can computerize them all.

By entering these transactions into a computerized database—with the right computer software this requires only a few keystrokes—the data are captured for rapid and freewheeling manipulations later on. For example, you can assign each transaction to an expense or income category, and in a flash have the computer print a summary from which it's easy to prepare your annual tax return.

By looking at your checks, charges, and cash payments during each calendar month, you can easily compare your actual to your budgeted expenses. You can find out if you paid that bill last month, or when your subscription to *City Magazine* expires. A computerized database of financial transactions provides you with an excellent tool for money management; it also lets you project your expenses far into the future. You could conceivably do all this manually, of course. But you probably wouldn't. With the computer, it's easy and fun!

By entering your stock and bond purchases, income (monthly or quarterly, taken from your account statements), and sales, you can use the computer to track your history as an investor. You can quickly identify your best and worst investments, and grasp the big picture of how your investment portfolio is aligned. You might even be able to have your computer draw a graph of it. By using the computer to see your cash, your stocks, your bonds, and so forth all at once, you can more easily decide to reallocate your money to take advantage of a current phase of the business cycle.

Develop Electronic Worksheets for Important Computations

Alongside your database and your word processing programs, another of your most important computer applications will be an electronic worksheet. It was the power of Visicalc, and later of Lotus 1-2-3, that brought personal computers into the office and the home. These and dozens of similar programs allow you to manipulate numbers, formulas, and sophisticated mathematical functions as easily as words. By writing the proper formula, you let the computer do all your addition, subtraction, multiplication, division, and other calculations in the wink of an eye. Even better, when you change the numbers in your electronic spreadsheet—say from "2 + 2" to "2 + 3"—the computer automatically recalculates all the relevant formulas and functions and gives you the new answers right away. This allows you to build an automatic calculator for almost any situation or business operation you can represent with numbers.

TAXES

Doing your quarterly or annual income tax returns—federal and state and perhaps local—is a cumbersome chore. But it's mostly mathematics. In fact, it's tailor-made for doing on an electronic spreadsheet.

Simple enter all the numbers and work all the math on your computer instead of on paper. Later, when you change the numbers for greater accuracy, or change the allocation of insurance or other overhead expenses, you simply enter the changes and let the computer redo the calculations. When the work is all done, simply print the worksheet and copy the numbers onto the proper tax forms.

BUSINESS BUDGETS AND PROPOSALS

Nearly all of budgeting and a great many proposals depend on mathematics and accounting. All of this work is far easier when done on an electronic spreadsheet.

What's particularly nice is you can allocate, say, 28 percent of a monthly income figure for a particular expense, then let the computer take care of calculating the dollar amount. As the monthly income figure changes, the computer automatically changes the corresponding dollar amounts.

With proposals, there's a tremendous opportunity to play "what if" games. What if the costs could be held to 10 percent? What if the price were $31.95 instead of $29.95? What if we sold 8,000 units instead of 7,500? To build a proposal or a budget that makes sense and wins acceptance, it's often important to "massage" the data to better reflect expectations, likelihood, and reality. On paper, this entails dozens and dozens of tries, as well as, tedious recalculations. On the computer, you build the budget or proposal model just once, then vary the critical figures and formulas until the answers come out the way you'd like them to.

Naturally, building an electronic model that looks good does not by itself guarantee success in the real world. But the electronic spreadsheet goes a long way toward simplifying, speeding up, and improving the accuracy of the development process that must take place before anyone will agree to initiate significant action.

THE IMPORTANCE OF DELEGATION

If you have absolutely no one to help you do anything, and if you plan never to have anyone help you, you can probably skip this section and not lose much. But for almost everyone else, delegation is an extremely valuable way to do more in less time. The guidelines for delegation give you a clear method for getting more done in less time by adding the energy of other people to your own.

But don't think for a minute that delegation is a way to shirk responsibility or get out from under a heavy work load. All it does is pyramid you and your efforts so you're in control of more than your own time. When you delegate, you gain influence over other people's time as well as your own. This gives you the responsibility of trying to use their time as well as you try to use your own.

Properly done, delegation not only saves you considerable time but obtains just as satisfactory results as doing the work yourself. But to delegate properly, you need a basic pattern. The following flowchart shows you the delegation process. Keep this in mind as you proceed.

Delegation Flowchart

Decide to delegate task

Select appropriate delegate

Describe desired results, resources, contacts, deadlines, and other factors to delegate

Listen to delegate's reaction

Negotiate delegation agreement

Agree on reporting method and schedule

Complete the project

Evaluate the project

Plan First

Poorly planned delegation is often wasted time. Before you initiate delegation, be sure of these important considerations:

a) Exactly what do you want that person (or delegate) to achieve, and how will both of you know when it is achieved?

b) Exactly how much room is there in this goal for modifications, additions, and deletions your delegate may want

to install? What are the reasons for any absolute limitations you decree?

c) Exactly what resources (materials, budget, experience,
and authority) can you give your delegate? With whom
should he or she work? In what relationship? Is all this
enough to achieve what you want? If not, what else has
to be gathered, and how?

d) Exactly how much leeway can you give your delegate to
implement his or her own ideas, plans, and methods on
the road to the designated achievement? (For best results, offer as much leeway as you can, and allow your
delegate to use as much or as little of this leeway as he
or she wants.)

e) Exactly what deadlines apply to this delegated assignment?

f) Exactly what role do you wish to play in reaching the
designated achievement? Why?

g) Exactly what method will you use to keep in touch with
your delegate's progress?

Do It Right the First Time

Once you know all this, you can start talking with your proposed
delegate and negotiate a satisfactory working agreement. That's
right: an agreement!

a) Can your delegate accept the goal you have in mind and
wholeheartedly work toward it? If not, can you reach
agreement on a goal you can both accept?

b) Can your delegate handle the assignment as it stands,
with the resources you can make available? Can he or she
work without you to gather whatever else may be
needed? Can your delegate work with the people required, and in the way required?

c) Is your delegate satisfied with the creative limits you are
imposing?

d) Does your delegate appear able to meet required deadlines on this assignment?

e) Is your delegate comfortable with the role you wish to

play? If not, can you reach agreement on a different role
for you?

f) Does your delegate understand the reporting process
you want to use on this assignment? Can you reach
agreement on crucial phases of the project so you can
time your progress-reporting schedule accordingly?

At one time, not too long ago, the popular belief was that delegation meant ordering someone to do exactly as you would do if only you had more time. But careful investigations seem to show that people produce better results if they have a hand in shaping and planning the project, and if they have room for using personal judgment in helping to carry it out.

In reality, delegates run the whole spectrum from Bob Cratchit to Tom Sawyer. And so do delegators. So you must modify the delegation process to meet whatever power and personal requirements may emerge. Any approach is okay, just so you both agree on certain minimum-performance parameters that are later met.

Delegate, Don't Dispose Of

Some kind of prearranged reporting process in all of the above will protect both you and your delegate during and after the delegation period. Progress reporting is an important part of delegation from several standpoints:

a) The formal reporting process ensures that you, as delegator, will keep in general touch with the project from start to finish. Put a note concerning each task you delegate in your Daily Prompter so you are automatically reminded to keep on top of its progress and problems.

b) The reporting process encourages your delegate to think of you as backup, and to come to you when events start moving too fast or head off in the wrong direction.

c) You have smartly geared the reporting schedule to lag a few days behind crucial events in the project's development. This way, if anything important goes wrong, you will find out about it fairly soon, either by way of the report or by the absence or postponement of a report that's due.

In addition to retaining certain responsibilities and receiving reports on a prearranged schedule, the good delegator plays backup. But draw the line between playing backup and playing nursemaid. When you play nursemaid, no one makes a move without you and you are far too indispensable to be out of touch for a moment. You haven't delegated here, you've merely taken on a few more arms and legs to direct.

When you play backup, you do not allow yourself to be buttonholed by surprise on your way out of your office, or laden with chores at any time. Instead, you are available by appointment only, to listen to your delegate's problems and to his or her suggested solutions. You help by asking questions, providing feedback, and offering encouragement where appropriate. In fact, a reliable indicator of how well you are delegating is who has the next move. If your delegate has it, you are on the right track. If you have delegated an assignment, but nevertheless the next move is yours, your delegation technique needs improvement.

Above and beyond negotiating, participating, and being involved in the formal reporting process, you retain final responsibility for what you delegate. Clearly, you can't get rid of something unpleasant merely by delegating it. Even more important: It's grossly unfair and often unethical for you to delegate certain of your responsibilities. Particularly in well-structured organizations, it's wrong to delegate within certain specific areas of your responsibility. These include:

a) Confidentiality. If the material involved is confidential, you should not allow a delegate to handle it for you.
b) Discipline. You must do your disciplining in person. Delegating this is both unfair and undesirable.
c) Morale. No one can replace you as morale officer. You must keep people motivated and forward-looking on your own.
d) Problems. It would be nice to have someone take your crises and emergencies off your hands, but they really belong to you. You can delegate certain specifics to others, but you should keep the overall lead. If someone solves your problems for you, you'll lose points. If you solve

them yourself, you'll gain. You'll even gain—
posthumously—if you go down with the ship.

Upgrade Through Delegation

One of the most common problems preventing good delegation is said to be a lack of well-trained, qualified people. The common refrain goes something like this: "I just don't have anyone I can delegate to." You may have joined this chorus yourself. But a lack of qualified people can reflect deeper, underlying problems. For example, in one Eastern big-city school district, the school board administrators were constantly pressured with too much to do and not enough people to whom they could delegate. They mouthed the standard complaint: lack of well-trained, qualified people. But on looking closer, a consultant began to see how the administrators' own poor delegation habits prevented their subordinates from acquiring the training and the qualifications needed. In some cases, administrators delegated so perversely that they, in effect, prevented the school board staff from using the training and qualifications they already possessed.

Delegation is most often thought of and used as a tool to unburden the boss from unwanted work and time demands. But it works equal wonders when used as a tool to teach, to provide experience and exposure to challenges that upgrade the people around you. In fact, these two uses go hand in hand.

For example, a typical overworked executive suddenly received authority to oversee considerably more of the operations within his organization. Since he was already working a full day, the only way to find time for the new activities was to slough off some of the old ones. Delegation was a good tool for this. In addition, the expansion of his authority put him in line for a move upward toward the company presidency. And that, he wisely realized, would never happen unless he had one or more subordinates groomed to take over his present place. Delegation was a good tool for this, too.

In another situation, a woman home all summer long with her children began training them to: straighten their own rooms, make and pour their own drinks, change clothes themselves, put dirty clothes in the laundry basket, and select their own menus from what was available in the house. These were tasks she could "delegate" to them, both as a means of making better use of her time and as a way to "upgrade" her children's skills and abilities.

The "open secret" behind getting good, qualified people to support your efforts is to make the people around you more experienced, knowledgeable, and skillful. You do this by giving them plenty of tough practice under your watchful eye. Delegation is one of the best tools for this kind of training. Here's a proven method that may work for you:

a) Organize all the tasks under your control in order of:
   1) importance, and 2) difficulty.
b) Cross off all the tasks now handled by other people, or otherwise not a time problem for you.
c) Of the tasks that remain, begin delegating them from the bottom of your list.
d) The first time you delegate a particular task to a particular person, contribute as much supervision and support as you feel that person will require to maximize his/her chances for success.
e) Each succeeding time you delegate the same task to the same person, slightly reduce your support and supervision. After a few trials, you will reach a stable, acceptable balance between the results he/she obtains and the amount of time you give to supervision and support.
f) Keep delegating more and more of the list until you have delegated everything, or you have saturated the people around you and they cannot handle one more delegated responsibility.

Incidentally, be sure to use the time you free up through delegation for the most useful, most valuable purposes you can find.

Grow Through Delegation

Most people have a strong tendency to retain activities from their past even when these well-practiced actions are no longer useful or (in some cases) appropriate to their present position. You tend to get used to certain tasks; you come to enjoy certain others.

And you keep giving time to them even though you have more important responsibilities. But as your life and work situations develop, these comfortable actions should generally give way to some of the newer tasks more appropriate to your position, skills, and abilities.

For example, a teacher was promoted to an administrative post in a very fine school district. But teaching was such a comfortable, habitual pattern of behavior that she spent a great deal of time on routine work with teachers. She went out of her way to analyze textbooks and supervise nearby classrooms because she was trying to relive her old job. Once she realized what her pattern of choices signified, though, she was able to delegate much of her classroom-related activities and replace them with new projects requiring her to learn new administrative skills.

Thus, you can accomplish this process of consciously growing through delegation by discarding old habits and tasks and using the freed-up time to take on new and more satisfying replacement responsibilities. Delegation makes the process easier because you continue to supervise your delegate(s), and so you tend to "cut the cord" more slowly. When asked to shed a task by quitting it abruptly, completely, and finally, you tend to balk. Delegation makes shedding such tasks more comfortable.

Schedule Your Delegation

While the delegation process generally gives you more time for your most important projects, the act of delegating can sometimes disrupt your day. For example, say you receive a letter, memo, or some other reminder of a project you want to accomplish. But in the interests of better effectiveness, you decide to delegate it. Here's what might happen. First, you immediately call for your delegate (disrupting his or her use of time). Then the two of you think through the assignment you want to delegate (wasting your time and more of your delegate's). Finally, you delegate the assignment in detail (spending time you could use more productively some other way). Even worse, you may repeat this pattern several times a day, wasting extra time on each occurrence.

The better way is to schedule a general "delegation period." When you recognize a task for someone else to handle, make an appointment with your delegate to discuss the assignment during your next delegation period. Then file the paperwork in your Daily Prompter. Wait until you have a few tasks to delegate, even if you're going to give them to several different people; you'll make better use of everyone's time if you schedule a single time for making all current assignments. This not only gives you an opportunity to think through the assignment(s), but also puts the act of delegation where you want it in your schedule—not just where it happens to pop up. If there is a rush, of course, you can make the appointment for later the same day. But most of the time, you can benefit from concentrating your delegation time.

MEETING MADNESS: HOW TO USE, EVALUATE, AND AVOID UNWANTED GATHERINGS

Meetings can be one of the most common—and best—methods of accomplishing any work. However, far too many meetings turn out to be boring, too lengthy, too crowded, and, worst of all, unproductive. Even if it accomplished a good deal, a meeting can occupy more time than it should. You can probably avoid all but 10 percent of your meetings without compromising your productivity. In fact, by using this extra time to good advantage, you can probably enhance it.

Unfortunately, organizational pressures and other restrictions may force you to attend more meetings than you would like. So be it. But attend them with the attitude that whether or not you are in control of a meeting, you can nearly always contribute in some measure to its smooth running and its effectiveness.

Speaking at Meetings

Whatever purpose they serve or agenda they follow, most meetings respond to good oration. The smooth talker can sway a meeting far more powerfully than the person with better ideas who lacks public speaking skill or experience. You can make better use of the time you spend at meetings if you practice and develop your oratorical skills:

a) *Caution:* Be sure brain is engaged before putting mouth

in gear. Know what you want to say before you speak. Unless you are a natural orator, you can nearly always benefit from planning what you will say.

b) Jot a list of key words on a tablet in front of you as a guide for what you want to say. In many meetings, you may not get the floor again for some time, so list each thought as it comes to you, then make all your relevant points when you have the chance to speak.

c) Use strong, persuasive talk to get the attention your ideas deserve. Don't bother with flowery phraseology or "housekeeping" comments such as: "In reply to what Mary said . . ." or "I know this has been said before, but I want to repeat it." (Of course, give credit to others, when due.)

d) Make your points with concrete examples, and be equally specific about the benefits you expect your ideas to bring the group. In general, anyone who can misunderstand you will almost certainly do so, but you can minimize misunderstandings if you stay with specifics.

e) Say what you intended to say, then stop. At the least, this tactic saves you some time and promotes a quick flow in the meeting. At best, your points seem more powerful and exert some "leadership by example" both for what you want and for how you would like the meeting to proceed.

Listening at Meetings

The other half of the meetings process is to listen. This means paying active attention to all of what each speaker says, means, and privately thinks as evidenced by all you know of him or her. Here are some useful techniques for listening at meetings:

a) Take brief notes on what each person says. Devote a whole page of your tablet, or a portion of the top page, to each attendee, depending on how much space you think you'll need. Then use codes, abbreviations, and key words to record the gist of what particular individuals say every time they speak. You can then review all their

comments to better understand their specific points of
view.

b) Since people speak slower than you can listen, use the
"extra" time between their words and sentences to analyze what they are saying. Listen for the meaning of
their words and for their motivation. Apply what you
know about people to their comments and look for
underlying ideas, attitudes, and feelings. This will help
you understand them better, and may help you find a
way to persuade them to do what you prefer.

Rating Your Meetings

The simple act of evaluating the quality and productivity of your
meetings improves every meeting that comes after. Here is a ten-
item evaluation chart for rating any meeting you attend. Give each
item a rating of 0 to 10 points depending on how well the meeting
fulfills it:

Rating

	0	1	2	3	4	5	6	7	8	9	10
1. Starts on time?											
2. Has an adequate written agenda?											
3. Everyone present and prepared?											
4. Follows written agenda in order, without digression or backtracking?											
5. Leader encourages participation?											
6. Plenty of discussion of important points, without repetition?											

7. General agreement by end of meeting?

8. Everyone clear regarding outcome of meeting, what each is to do as a result of meeting, and when he/she is to do it?

9. Agenda completed?

10. Ends on time?

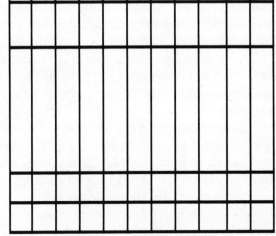

Keep completed scorecards as a record of your meeting experiences.

RATING YOUR MEETING LEADERS

If you rate a lot of meetings run by the same few people, you may begin to notice that those run by certain individuals consistently score higher than those run by others. This is almost certainly a sign of their skill. You can begin to make your own meetings more effective by asking some of the highest scorers to run the important meetings you call or control, or by patterning your own group leadership after these top performers.

Calculating the Cost of Your Meetings

Many people enjoy meetings so much they convene them for little or no reason. For example, businesses very often hold regular "department meetings" even when there is nothing important to discuss, or a decision maker will call a meeting to get five people's help in making a simple choice. Some people use meetings the way some baseball players use chewing tobacco: as a habit. In my experience, you need strong reasons to deter these people from their chosen pastime. And one very strong reason can be the prohibitive cost of a meeting that doesn't produce much of value. You may not be able to get such people to dislike meetings in general, but you can get them to think twice about calling one particular meeting if you point out what it will cost in comparison to its likely benefits.

The clearest and easiest situation is where consultants or experts are called in for a meeting. They bill for their time, so you can try to compare the cost of the meeting against the value of what it produces.

In situations where everyone is an employee, there are no special dollar expenditures for the attendees' time. Nevertheless, the same principle holds. Everyone's time has value, if only because he or she should spend it doing the most valuable task in the hopper. In this case, dollar figures simply provide the lowest common denominator for comparing the values of otherwise dissimilar tasks.

You calculate the cost of a meeting very simply:

a) Get the (contemplated or actual) attendance list. Calculate the rough hourly rate for every attendee. A person's hourly rate roughly equals their annual salary plus overhead (usually about as much as the annual salary) divided by 2,000 (the approximate number of hours people work in a year). You can express this mathematically as: $2 \times \text{salary} \div 2{,}000 = \text{rough hourly rate}$.

b) Add up the rough hourly rates for all the attendees to find the rough hourly cost of the meeting.

c) Multiply the probable length of the meeting, in hours, by its rough hourly cost to find the approximate total cost.

Now compare this cost with the benefits likely to result from the meeting. How you calculate these benefits will depend in large measure on the meeting's purpose. However, you can begin comparing the cost with the likely benefits by thinking along the following lines:

a) What will the results be if this meeting never takes place? Will the anticipated results to be produced by the meeting justify the extra cost of holding it?

b) Can we shorten the meeting to improve its anticipated cost/benefit ratio?

Is the meeting worthwhile? If so, hold it with confidence. If not, find some other, less time-consuming way to accomplish the same results.

Learning How to Avoid Meetings

Meetings serve a multitude of purposes. Most obviously, they let people make direct contact with each other. This in turn leads to other important interactions: the exchange of ideas and attitudes, the stimulation of thought and feeling, the sizing up of other people, and the establishing of personal relations.

However, many people call and attend far too many meetings in relation to what their meeting time accomplishes. You'll be far more efficient and productive if you know how to avoid the unnecessary or unwarranted meetings. You can use four basic techniques to avoid meetings:

a) Use telephones in place of meetings to keep in close contact with other people. This helps spur many of the interactions that meetings would promote. You may be able to accomplish quite a few of your purposes without a meeting.

b) Use written communication in place of meetings to get across ideas and information. This works particularly well to replace "news conferences," or any meetings called to spread information rather than to make decisions or share ideas. You can fruitfully replace many routine meetings—or portions of meetings—with a written report or summary.

c) Delegate your attendance. This technique does nothing to prevent the meeting; it simply pulls you out of it. Instead of attending in person, you send someone who: 1) says and asks what you intended to say and ask in person, and 2) reports to you what other people said and, in particular, what they answered in response to your questions.

d) Substitute idea books for so-called "thinking sessions." Many times people call meetings to thrash out ideas—to "brainstorm," to "bounce ideas around"—in an effort to solve problems or originate actions. I firmly believe in such meetings, but sometimes you can use an idea book instead to save time or eliminate one too many meetings.

The idea book is a plain notebook, titled with the purpose of the meeting it replaces. You leave the book somewhere accessible, so everyone who would have been invited to the meeting can spend time with it. Everyone on the list: a) regularly enters his or her thoughts, ideas, suggestions, and comments in the notebook, and b) reads what all others have written before making new entries. Over a period of a few days or weeks, the idea book blossoms out with the same ideas and exchanges that might have occurred in a meeting. Sometimes, it produces even better results because the elapsed time between each person's entries gives him or her time to consider many factors more fully. However, the black-and-white nature of an entry in an idea book may inhibit some people. That why it's important to keep the idea book as free and open as a brainstorming session: no criticisms, no judgments at first. Only after people have found a good number of options and alternatives should the idea book be thrown open for criticism, evaluation, and the transformation of the first set of entries into something practical and useful.

One-on-One Meetings

Talks with one other person are not generally recognized as "meetings," but they contain many of the same time-wasting dangers, and they respond to many of the same useful techniques. Make sure your one-on-one meetings:

a) Have time limits, and start and end on time.
b) Have agendas and specific purposes. Make sure one or

both of you have the resources, information, authority, and anything else you need to accomplish the meeting's purposes. If you don't, the meeting is a waste of time.

c) End with both of you in agreement on what was accomplished, if anything. Without such agreement, chances are: 1) the meeting did not accomplish what you or the other person thought it did, and 2) you'll have to hold another meeting to clarify and redo the events of this meeting. It's obviously more effective to accomplish your purposes this first time.

Meetings for Planning

Meetings organized to plan an event or action require special handling to keep them running on track and working effectively. These meetings emphasize thought over action in the review of situations, circumstances, and potential objectives. This means you must discuss issues, problems, opportunities, and repercussions at great length with people representing all parts of the plan and interested in all sorts of special factors. The culmination of the meeting can be very abstract, often nothing more than a series of reference points against which to measure any possible plan. Because the planning process is cumbersome enough without gumming it up unnecessarily, you'll want to streamline your planning sessions with these methods:

a) Invite only those who can bring to the plan such necessary items as: authority, resources, and/or elements needed for implementation. Include those people with the expertise to verify that your tentative plans are workable. Otherwise, grandiose but uninformed thinkers will make plans that are tough to implement. And it works in reverse, too. Planning committees often get stuck, while anyone with the right experience knows four separate ways to do a job fast, right, and inexpensively.

b) Select a meeting leader powerful enough to control the people in attendance, but democratic enough to facilitate everyone's involvement. A planning meeting is not worthy of its name if one person "runs" it and forces his or her plan on everyone else.

c) Make the first item on the agenda the formulation of the plan's purpose: its goal. Once people agree on this, they can evaluate every aspect of the plan in terms of its contribution to or detraction from this purpose.

d) If the plan becomes unwieldy, encourage everyone in the meeting to review the agreed-upon purpose and look for a simpler way to achieve it. In general, the simplest plans are the best.

e) Spend as much time as it takes to get a useful, workable plan. While this process may require extra meetings and delay the start of the project, a well-thought-out plan saves you and everyone else involved a great deal more time and effort when you try to put it into action.

Action Meetings

The action meeting can be anything from an envelope-stuffing party to a political caucus, from a friend helping you exchange sports car engines to a board of directors struggling for power in a penthouse suite. In such a meeting, the emphasis is on the results you can achieve. To make your action meeting more successful and effective:

a) Invite only those who can move things forward or, by withholding their cooperation, slow things up. Too many people in the meeting will confuse everyone and create no time-saving or performance-improving benefit.

b) Select a strong meeting leader who can delegate assignments, make decisions quickly, and keep attendees focused on development and implementation of the action plan.

c) Start the agenda with a brief review of the purpose of the meeting and the steps required to reach it. Once everyone understands the purpose at hand, he or she can work more effectively toward this common goal.

While you should nearly always tell the people working with you what you want to achieve, you must be a little more discreet in some circumstances than in others.

A political caucus is an example of a meeting where it is not always productive or effective to announce your plan. One reason is that the meeting's purpose involves more negotiation than simple action. Some of the people at the meeting are going to act, and others are going to react, often in unpredictable ways. To help ensure that your meeting achieves what you want, you may find it fruitful to hold two meetings: first, a private meeting with your team at which you go over your agenda, specify your objectives, and make tentative work assignments; then, the working session, in which the negotiation or action actually takes place.

d) Accept the fact that few plans are carried out to perfection. In the heat of action, you will almost certainly have to settle for less than you want in some parts of the plan. In other portions of it, you may have to invent whole new ways to achieve the results you expect. And in some cases, you may have to abandon the plan entirely and improvise as best you can.

News Meetings

These are announcements, briefings, and, to an extent, training sessions where the main thrust of communication is from the leader or a designated speaker to a theoretically receptive audience. To handle these meetings well, you must:

a) Formulate completely and clearly the information, attitudes, and ideas you want to convey.
b) Develop a plan for conveying what you want as clearly, accurately, and concisely as possible.
c) Use whatever technology and techniques you need to get your message(s) across effectively. This means exposing your audience to rich sensory material, including: spoken words, music, pictures, film, animation, sound effects, items to handle and feel, written information, smells, tastes, or ideas that grab the imagination and perhaps even excite the libido.

d) Repeat your message at least three times: once in an introduction, once in detail, and once in a summary. Repeat it in three formats if you can: speech, visuals, and printed text. Research data show that people absorb very little of what they experience, and retain only a small portion of what they first absorb. One key to communication is, therefore, repetition. You can almost never repeat a message too often. You can almost never repeat a message too often. You can almost never repeat a message too often! The trick is to do it without boring your audience into inattention.

Surprise Meetings

These are more commonly known as interruptions. Your first reaction should be to avoid them. Refuse to be interrupted, or if you accept the interruption, refuse to spend more than three to five minutes away from what you were doing. But sometimes the interruption is worthwhile: An old college chum pops in on a one-day visit to your city, or a relative calls you with bad news or with a sweepstakes victory! Whatever the interruption, if you agree to participate in it, at least recognize you're in another meeting. Then use whichever techniques seem best suited to maximizing your effectiveness at the moment.Here are three good ones:

a) At the earliest possible moment, establish time limits, along with an agenda or purpose. Because this meeting is a surprise, you cannot start it on time. But you can certainly set a limit and end it on time. Do so.
b) Make sure the meeting is viable—that the people and resources available are sufficient to accomplish whatever purpose you have established. If the needed resources aren't available, consider ending the meeting, or cutting it short, and rescheduling for a better time.
c) Stick to your purpose. Resist digressions, discouragement, or efforts to start a new agenda before you complete the original one.

PLANNING AS A PROD TO PRODUCTIVITY

Making Successful, Specific Plans: For a Group and for Yourself

Planning is crucial to increased effectiveness, doing more, and shaping your results to meet your goals. It is the mechanism that lets you get out from under the crush and constant flow of events. Good planning puts you in the driver's seat instead of under the rear wheels. And best of all, good planners are made, not born. Nearly anyone can become a better planner simply by following the right principles and techniques. Try them, and you'll find this to be true.

PLANNING TEAMWORK

The planning you do for working with other people goes through the same stages as the planning you do for working alone:

a) Put your goals in order.
b) Develop a master plan.
c) Establish specific steps.
d) Schedule the steps in the best order.
e) Follow your schedule.

INVOLVEMENT

There are some important differences between working alone and working with others. Most notably: If you want to maintain maximum effectiveness, you must involve people in every stage of the planning process and incorporate their values, goals, and ideas into your final plan. While many people view this sharing as a loss of power, the involvement strategy actually has several very positive effects.

This involvement should start at the very beginning of planning. To get people involved and eager to contribute, you must allow them a fair amount of influence over the selection of goals. It's inevitable that in situations where you merely dictate goals and then expect others to attain them for you, you will sacrifice a great deal of motivation, ingenuity, creativity, and outright effort.

If you own and operate a small business, though, or you clearly control a small organization or group, you may be able to play a slightly more autocratic role. In situations where your leadership is well recognized and well accepted, it may be okay for you to lay down a specific goal as a means of establishing a common starting point.

COMPLEXITY

Planning for fast, efficient, productive work by a group is nearly always a complex undertaking that involves considerable effort to achieve. When you work alone, your plans must account only for the amount of work you can accomplish. For a work group of five, however, your plans must cover five times the volume of work, as well as five times the information, communication, and activity. In addition, someone must coordinate some or all of the two-person, three-person, and four-person relationships that develop within the group.

GREATER PLANNING POWER

Even though the group has a greater need for planning, it has greater power in this area. A work group of five must allow for more work, but it also has five planners who can develop comprehensive and successful steps to direct and control their group effort. The involvement strategy actually relieves you of some leadership burdens while making the planning process and the resulting work process more satisfying for everyone involved.

Experience 13

Self-Evaluation: Organizing Goals

Instructions: In your personal notebook, copy some of your more important goals from Experience 2, Experience 6, and Experience 9. Number them first in order of importance, then again in order of urgency, then a third time in order of their value to you, then a fourth time in order of their degree of challenge to you. When you are done, put them in overall order, with the one you will feel best about accomplishing ranked number 1.

Experience 14

Checking the Time You Save by Planning

Instructions: In your personal notebook, use a fresh page to follow this simple process for calculating the specific amount of time you save by planning projects before you start work on them.

1) Before you start work on your next four new projects, write down for each one the goal, objective, or result you hope to achieve. Next, write down a solid estimate of the time required to complete each one with your conventional (nonplanning or limited-planning) approach. You needn't pick four projects you'll work on simultaneously. It's okay to conduct this "experiment" over whatever period it takes to complete four. You can even apply the process to six or eight projects, if you prefer. It's important to do at least four, however, so you have a solid basis for comparison. For some people, it's too easy to underestimate the time required and thus fail to realize the time savings inherent in planning before you take action.

2) Now take time to develop a solid plan for accomplishing the first and the third of these goals, objectives, or results. After you have developed a plan for the project, note the total amount of time you spent planning it.

3) Now work on the projects. For the second and fourth projects, get to work after your usual amount of planning. For the first and third, put your plan into action. As you complete each project, note the total amount of time you spent working on it. Get this figure from a Time Log (explained in Appendix A) or a project diary you kept for this purpose. Exclude the planning time you listed in item 2 above.

4) Now compare. Make appropriate allowances for differ-

ences in scope or difficulty of the various projects you've included in this experiment. Compare the time to plan and complete a project with the time needed to finish it (or an equivalent project) without a plan. The more often you try planning before taking action, the more likely you are to be convinced of the effectiveness of this strategy.

PLANNING TIME MULTIPLIES ITSELF

"Cast your bread upon the waters, and it shall return tenfold." (Ecclesiastes 11:01)

To prove the truth of this with regard to planning, go through the simple instructions of Experience 14. You'll usually find that taking the time to plan saves about twice as much time as you spend. Thus, for every hour of planning, you generally save two hours of implementation. You can save even more on complex projects. Even though you give a good slice of your time to planning, your start-to-finish time for a project will be considerably less when you make planning your first major step.

PRACTICE YOUR PLANNING

Planning skills are like any others: They grow rusty with disuse; sharper, the harder you work them. So before you mow the lawn, plan how you'll do it. Before you drive to the store, plan your route and your shopping list. Before you take your vacation, develop a detailed vacation itinerary. You'll save thirty seconds here, a few minutes there, as much as an hour or two on projects, as you plan your way through your work and your life. Don't fret that this may be frivolous. Your planning skills will steadily develop, and carry over to the most important areas of your work and your life. Net result: You'll multiply your total effectiveness and productivity tremendously.

Just gaining the extra time may seem enough benefit for you to plan much or nearly all of what you do. But there's a bigger benefit, too: The development of powerful planning skills will allow you to take control of your life today, this week, this month, this year, and beyond. Understand that you will never receive anything like this:

> *You are cordially invited to include some of your Long-Range Goals and Immediate Objectives in today's and this week's Regular Plans. The favor of your action is respectfully requested.*

No one I know issues such *engraved invitations* to help you achieve your goals. Nevertheless, some people I have met indeed seem to be waiting for such strong encouragement to put more useful principles, ideas, and techniques to work in their lives. Please don't be one of them. Issue your own invitation, and say "Yes" right now. Watch how easily it can happen!

Daily, Weekly, Monthly, Yearly Planning

Your Daily Prompter is a good tool for implementing your daily, weekly, and monthly plans. Use it to cue you with the items you have previously set aside to accomplish each day, week, and month. If you prefer, you can use the scheduling ideas in Appendix B instead. The basic point is to plan. Use the planning process to break down every desired accomplishment into a series of specific tasks. Schedule these tasks, then do them. You'll find the same few planning steps make up the entire process, and you can apply them again and again to plan the largest project, the smallest chore, and every task in between.

DAILY PLANNING

Every day of your life, decide: a) what you want to accomplish this day, b) your priorities for these accomplishments, and c) what you can do to achieve them. Ideally, you'll tackle the highest-priority accomplishment with the most direct task you can find. You'll work on this as long as you can, or until you complete it, then move on to the next highest priority.

But don't overplan. Fill your schedule with the most important items, but leave 20 to 50 percent of your time unscheduled. This allows for sudden shifts in priority, new tasks, and surprise items that disrupt your original plans. You may notice that a well-planned day can uncrowd your desk. With every project and task accounted for, you don't need piles of paper to remind you what is pending. In fact, when one well-planned day follows another in a long series, you will find very few projects get lost, fall behind, or remain pending very long.

WEEKLY PLANNING

Follow the same procedure week to week. Every Friday or Monday morning, for example, take thirty minutes to plan the coming week's work. Set up the goals you would like to accomplish, then establish plans for reaching them. Sort your week's goals into day-by-day accomplishments, handling each day's work as it comes up in your schedule. If you like, you can plan your weekends this way, too.

MONTHLY PLANNING

Follow the same procedure month to month. Use an hour or so of the last week each month to plan your accomplishments for the coming month. Sort your monthly goals into week-by-week accomplishments, then break these down further as they appear in your schedule. With your regular plans, it's vital to include some of the items that will help you achieve the long-range personal and career goals you have established.

YEARLY PLANNING

Just as financial controllers assign dollar figures to every item in an Annual Budget, you can assign time allotments to every item in your Yearly Plan. And in fact, this is one of the best ways I know to make sure you find time for those most important but easily delayed projects you wish you could get to.

For example, a young lawyer had the idea of buying a cabin in the woods and fixing it up as a hunting lodge and vacation home. But year after year, something always came up to delay the project. Finally, I gave him the idea of the Yearly Plan and its Annual Time Budget. He entered his cabin into his Yearly Plan, assigned it several weekends' worth of work, and forgot it. But when the designated weekends came up on his calendar, this young man determined to follow his Plan. He pulled himself away from the "something" that had come up and went off exploring for his cabin. By the end of the year, he owned a cabin that pleased him and his family, and was well along in his plans to fix it up for regular use.

These are the steps to make a Yearly Plan work for you:

a) Include all the long-range projects you want to achieve.
b) Allocate each one a fair amount of time: enough to make steady progress toward meeting the deadline you assigned the project.
c) Make specific time assignments so you know exactly:
   1) what dates you will work on each of these projects,
   2) what you will try to accomplish on each of these dates, and 3) how much time you will spend on each designated date.
d) Follow your Yearly Plan.

It helps if you mark the Plan, or at least the designated dates, on the calendar you consult most often. Then, keep the written Plan handy, reviewing it frequently to note your progress, prepare for the next stage, and keep the importance of it firmly in mind.

MAKING USE OF TRAVEL TIME

Most of the time you spend traveling is not physically demanding. Even while walking, you can carry useful items, think useful thoughts, and carry on a fruitful conversation. While driving, you can listen to tapes, think, and talk out loud to yourself or on the car telephone to others. On trains, boats, or planes, you're usually free to read, write, think, and talk. All this translates into the potential to make good use of travel time.

Five-Minute Tasks

These are the basis for much of your effectiveness during actual travel time. A five-minute task is a self-contained task you can pick up, understand, and accomplish in five or ten minutes. Tasks that require special equipment or reference to specialized sources of information do not qualify as five-minute tasks, because they are not self-contained. However, modern dictation equipment and portable reference sources (print and electronic) vastly increase the range of tasks you can do on the run.

For example, the task of compiling a list of rug-cleaning firms in your neighborhood might not be a five-minute task, since it may require you to carry a heavy phone book or directory with you. But if you can photocopy the pages you need and carry them with you, you have transformed this chore into a five-minute task you can do on the run. I know an auto-leasing salesperson who carries a portable computer and printer with him as he makes his sales calls. Anywhere there is a telephone, he can call his home office and go to work. Even without a telephone, he can do calculations and print the "boiler plate" for leases. In just five minutes, he and his equipment can turn out a neatly typewritten contract specifying every aspect of any proposed lease. This creates many portable five-minute tasks out of what used to be thirty-minute chores done with secretarial help at the home office.

Other five-minute tasks include: general reading, routine writing assignments, thinking over situations you have previously studied, making decisions between alternative choices you have previously researched, making notes on your last appointment, boning up on details for your next appointment, and so forth.

Five-minute tasks not only keep you productive, they keep you flexible. You can take a break almost whenever you want. You have only to finish the task in front of you to be free with no loose ends. And you can choose from among all your five-minute tasks the ones that suit your mood, capacities, or available resources. These benefits give five-minute tasks significant advantages over longer projects, where you may need fifteen to thirty minutes just to set up to work, and where you cannot afford to quit or take a break for fear of losing your place or having to redo much of what you have already accomplished.

Once you begin to look for five-minute tasks, you will see plenty of them all around you. Save enough of them to keep you busy while you travel.

The Portable Office

This refers to a slim-line briefcase or other convenient container you use as your portable office whenever you travel. You put in all the essential equipment you need to get results on the run. Here are some tips on how you can furnish your own portable office:

a) Collect useful chores, challenges, or five-minute tasks
   you can do while you travel to and from your main project sites. If your travel pattern is fairly well set, you will
   know approximately how much travel time you can devote to five-minute tasks every day. Be prepared with
   this much work. In fact, store your five-minute tasks in
   your portable office so you are always ready to work en
   route. You can keep a work schedule or inventory of all
   your pending tasks right in your portable office to help
   you organize and control your work.

b) Invest in equipment for your portable office, such as a
   portable recorder for dictation, a portable cassette
   player, or a portable telephone. These help you make the
   best use of your travel time. One man purchased a
   computer with a cellular data phone for his portable office to make writing and electronic messaging much easier. Another traveler established a steady supply of
   worthwhile material on prerecorded tapes, educational
   programs from which he could benefit, and even novels
   and business books to make his travel time more fruitful.

Using Your Seat as a Desk

Almost all commercial travel time is taken up with sitting: while
going by car to the station or airport, waiting for the train or
plane, actually taking the journey, going by car from the station
or airport to your destination, and the same sequence in reverse.
If you will carry enough five-minute tasks with you when you
travel, you can make all this travel time tremendously effective.

You can also make better use of the rest of your travel time if
you use your sitting time to plan ahead. Instead of working on
specific items, you review your itinerary, expand it or change it,
then prepare for what's ahead. The more of your trip you plan,
the more effective you will be. But it takes experience to know just
how much you can ask yourself to do. Experiment to find the right
amount: enough so you accomplish a great deal in each twenty-
four-hour period, but not so much you exhaust yourself and must
sacrifice some results to achieve others.

Using Long-Distance Travel Time

Long-distance travel usually gives you large blocks of time—
often two or three consecutive hours, or the equivalent to a week's
worth of open time at home. In addition, long-distance travel iso-
lates you from your family, friends, and common interruptions,
and it brings you fewer personal distractions and demands to pull
you away from making good use of your time. Whether you're on
the go 50 percent of your time or travel infrequently, you'll find
these techniques and strategies helpful in making good use of this
precious travel time:

a) Before you leave, line up the important work or thinking you will do on your journey. You can either schedule
   as many important items as you think you can handle, or
   devote yourself to one superimportant project. If you
   pick this second strategy, you will allocate all your travel
   time (one-way or round-trip) to this superimportant
   project you select.
b) Assemble the materials you will need in a briefcase or
   other accessible carry-on bag. Be sure to include writing
   materials, calculators, or any other equipment or resources your tasks require.
c) Get a fast start. On each portion of your journey, find a
   good seat and get settled quickly. As soon as you're settled, open your bag and start working. Have a timer
   with you or a clock in view so you can count down to
   the next time you're scheduled to change seats (from
   waiting room to airplane, or wherever).
d) Wait until the last minute to break off your efforts. Then
   stuff your work into your carry-on bag and move along.
   Time yourself to make the last call for passengers so you
   can work the few extra minutes before you board a plane
   or train. You can also be the last one off at your destination.
e) Keep working on your important tasks or project at
   every opportunity until you complete it or run out of
   travel time. And remember, your successful completion
   of travel-time work entitles you to relax and celebrate.
   Don't be shy about rewarding yourself for good accom-

plishments, because this helps assure you'll work just as hard next time you travel.

FASTER THAN A SPEEDING BULLET

Here are some tips to help you slide through your itinerary in less time than you thought possible.

a) Prepack once and then leave the suitcase, ready to go. If you travel more than 15 percent of your time, or if you travel more than twice a year on short notice, a prepacked bag is worth its weight in gold. Prepack a duplicate of all your everyday toiletries, underwear, eyeglasses, medicines, and whatever else you take on a trip. Then the day you leave, just add the appropriate outer clothes and you're ready.

b) Develop a relationship with a good travel agent, then "delegate" your booking chores. Travel agents do it better than you, as long as you tell them exactly what you want. And their services don't cost you a dime.

c) Leave copies of your itinerary at home and/or with colleagues. Check in with family and friends at least once a day, particularly if you feel some of your plans are uncertain or subject to change.

d) Keep extra money for travel ready in your wallet or purse: a traveler's check and/or a blank personal check will also be valuable. Your hotel will cash this for you if you run short but can't get to a bank.

e) For international travel, make sure to have the local currency in your pocket when you arrive. You can usually exchange some money while waiting to leave the previous country. This saves time at the airport or railway exchange booth, where tourists always form long lines. And later you'll get a better exchange rate at a large bank closer to your hotel.

f) If you fly frequently, join one of the airline lounge clubs. They make the time you spend in airports more comfortable and productive, and eliminate waiting on many lines.

g) Fly direct when possible. Flights that stop en route usu-

ally add between thirty minutes and two hours to your
flight time. Extra landings and takeoffs also increase your
chances of encountering equipment problems and other
delays.

h) Use carry-on luggage as much as possible. Checked baggage means a twenty- to forty-minute delay at your destination, and will almost certainly create an even longer
delay at least once in a while.

i) Watch for faster transportation. Sometimes an express
train or a nonstop flight leaves a little later but arrives
sooner than your first choice for transportation. Even if
you must spend a little extra money, you can sometimes
save a great deal of time.

Using Local Travel Time

Local travel time is sometimes harder to use well than travel time
more distant from your home base. First, you usually have more
local travel time, and you can run out of useful ways to fill it.
Second, during local travel you are more likely to be driving or
concerned with making your connections, rather than sitting as a
passenger on one long hop. It's harder to concentrate on anything
other than the travel. Nevertheless, you can be extremely effective
during local travel time if you make use of it as consistently and
frequently as possible. Here's how:

a) Make it a policy to use as much of your local travel time
as you can. Local travel time usually offers very short opportunities for reading, writing, thinking, or planning.
It's easy to say, "Well, never mind this opportunity, I'll
take advantage of the next one!" But this attitude allows
you to waste nearly all your opportunities. Instead, try
to make some good use of nearly every free travel moment. These more valuable minutes will soon add up to
many more valuable hours.

b) Plan good routes for your local travel hops and stick to
them. Once you establish your travel patterns, you can
pay much less attention to the mechanics of getting there
and concentrate more on accomplishing something
useful.

c) Instead of using your car, consider taking taxies, limousines, or public transportation for all or part of your local travel. Anything you can do to free your mind from routine chores will convert presently wasted travel time to highly productive hours.
d) Share your travel time. Car pooling or ride sharing is a great tool for doing this. The people who travel with you can contribute to your knowledge, stimulation, and effectiveness if you all participate in a combined effort to make good use of your travel time.

A Los Angeles college student has formed a car pool with classmates. Every day, one of the riders takes a turn lecturing on an agreed-upon topic. The half hour "lost" on the ride to school becomes a "found" study period that directly produces better grades and more free time at home.

Scheduling for Efficient Travel

The great-circle route is the shortest distance between two points on the globe. While you may not want an authentic great-circle route for all of your travel, the concept is a big help to your effectiveness. The idea is to save up your trips so you have several destinations each time you leave your home or office, then plan your route to touch all your destinations with a minimum of backtracking and redundant mileage. This kind of scheduling makes the average travel minute more effective because it reduces your total travel time without reducing results. And it works whether you're traveling thousands of miles by air, or less than a mile by bicycle. To schedule your own "great circles":

a) Look at or visualize a map of the region whenever you plan your routes. (Mark your most frequent destinations right on your maps so they're easier to find next time you look.)
b) Follow the fastest, not necessarily the shortest, route between destinations. For example, the direct road from one destination to another may be a slow crawl with red lights at every corner. You may make better time by go-

ing three miles farther along back roads that move faster. The only valid exceptions might be walking or bicycle routes you choose not for speed but for avoiding tiring hills or dangerous pathways.

c) Stay flexible. Be ready to change your route in mid-journey if conditions or priorities change.

Tips for Reducing Waiting Time

a) Schedule whatever you must do for off-peak hours. Eat lunch at 1 or 2 P.M., "hole up" in cities during the rush hours, check out of hotels early, or pick up tickets or other items at odd hours.

b) Hire a "line waiter": In many cities, you can find services that will provide people to wait on line for you. This is an inexpensive way to save time. They can actually transact your business at the head of the line, or call you so you can arrive in time to do it yourself.

c) Before you stop to wait on a line, try to reschedule your day so you can keep busy for now and come back when there may not be one. If you cannot reschedule, at least use five-minute tasks or other techniques to accomplish something useful during your waiting time.

d) Avoid bank lines entirely. Do all your banking by mail, or by teller machine at unusual hours. Also, spend as little cash as possible, and get what cash you need from stores, hotels, and others with whom you do business.

e) Avoid buying in person, particularly during sales or busy seasons. You can buy more than 50 percent of the merchandise you want via mail order, catalog sales, and telephone calls to your favorite stores. If you see something you like, write down the information, then call later and have it delivered. Get in the habit of shopping by phone as much as possible and you'll cut hours of waiting time out of your schedule.

f) Make appointments to the minute with everyone, including your hair stylist, doctor, dentist, and other people, too. When you call to make your appointment, explain that you're busy and trying to operate on a tight schedule. Offer to show up exactly on time for your appointment, but ask to be served immediately. Since there may still be some delays, bring five-minute tasks with you and make use of the time wasted in waiting rooms.

THE POWER OF PROCRASTINATION

If you're like most people, you consider procrastination to be a bad habit and a sure route to inefficiency. But procrastination has some positive aspects you don't want to overlook. Seen from the proper perspective, procrastination is actually a powerful tool that can greatly improve your productivity and level of achievement. But like any tool, it cuts both ways. If you lose control of your procrastination, you can face new problems you otherwise might not see.

The Power of Procrastination for Harm

Procrastination's greatest potential evil is that it may prevent you from accomplishing a particular goal. Like the members of the Procrastinators' Club of America (yes, one exists and, decades after its founding, has yet to hold its first meeting), you may fall years behind in doing important tasks or accomplishing significant goals. Like an airline schedule, when you fall behind in doing one item on your list, the delay can snowball to affect all the other items, too.

More common than a total failure to accomplish a goal, however, is a significant compromise on quality. Let's say you have a task that will normally take you four hours to finish, and it's due by the end of the day. If you start working on it a few hours later than you should, you won't be able to finish on time. You'll be tempted to rush through it, to cut corners, and to deliver something less than your best work. At the same time, you feel pressured by the fast-approaching deadline. You may enjoy the feeling of pressure, but many people prefer to avoid it whenever possible.

Perhaps the most frustrating aspect of procrastination is that it doesn't improve anything. When you put off a project, it rarely goes away; instead, it hangs over your head and ruins your effectiveness for, or enjoyment of, other projects and activities. When you finally turn to the task you've put off, it may have become more difficult to accomplish. Even if the situation is no worse, the task is usually more onerous because the pressure of time is added to the other unpleasant aspects of the chore.

The Power of Procrastination for Good

Imagine that your boss provides you with a complex assignment that involves making projections or decisions based on fast-changing factors, such as interest rates, supplier prices, the availability of good workers, the state of existing projects, or the like. If you were to be an eager beaver and make those projections or decisions today, you could be in trouble, because the situation might change significantly between now and the time the boss commits to a course of action. To provide the most current information, you might wind up doing the work again. Or you could let stand your out-of-date projections and take a chance that decisions based on them might look silly or work out badly.

A smarter, more effective alternative would be to rely on the positive power of procrastination. Taking this option, you wait patiently until the Latest Feasible Starting Date, then begin your work. If you time it right, you finish just before your boss must actually commit to a course of action. By procrastinating appropriately, you guarantee that your work is insulated from many of the interim changes in the fast-changing factors that control the situation. On project after project, your information, understanding, and analysis are always up to the minute because they're fresh.

Positive procrastination works even better with creative activities. If you write an advertisement or paint a picture well before you must deliver it, you have plenty of time to second-guess your creative instincts. Because you're not under much time pressure, you'll quite likely take too long to do the work, then require extra time to redo it, revise it, update it, or simply worry about whether it's good enough. Rather than turn your creative energies to the next project, you'll worry over the present project like a dog with a bone. You may never finish. Even if you do, you may obtain far less satisfaction and acceptance because you've unduly filtered the creative work through your intellect and your "critical self."

But if you procrastinate until the delivery date approaches, your creative mind will "cook" the assignment thoroughly before you write the first word or make the first stroke. Your work will likely be more "mature," potentially better, and certainly less damaged by your own second-guessing after you complete it.

Another positive feature of procrastination is its tendency to teach you calmness. While others are frantically working on a task, you coolly calculate the Latest Feasible Starting Date for the project. As you gain the confidence that you'll finish on time, you become less upset by time pressure. After years of procrastinating tasks for *positive* reasons, you'll be better able to remain calm in any kind of difficult situation.

How to Control Your Use of Procrastination

Clearly, there are positive as well as negative aspects to procrastination. The difficulty, of course, is making sure you benefit from the positive aspects without getting hurt by the negative ones.

The key to controlling your use of procrastination is to understand your motives for putting off a project. If you're avoiding a task because it's boring, unpleasant, difficult, or frightening, you're probably procrastinating for negative reasons. However, if you're putting off the task because you have more important things to do, or you're waiting for the Latest Feasible Starting Date, you're probably procrastinating for positive reasons.

To check, go through Experience 15.

Experience 15

Evaluating Reasons for Procrastination

Instructions: In your personal notebook, write down one or more projects that you are procrastinating. Then for each one, write down the answers to the following true-or-false statements:

1) I know how to do this project.
2) I look forward to doing this project.
3) I expect to enjoy working on this project.

4)   I have the time and energy to work on this project.
5)   I look forward to completing this project.
6)   It is too early to start work now and finish on time.
7)   Other projects now occupying my time are more important.

Evaluation: Every answer of "false" may signal a negative reason for procrastination. One or two "false" answers are a warning signal. Three or four "false" answers are a danger sign, and you should consider carefully whether or not to begin work on this project immediately. Five or more "false" answers are a strong indication that you are procrastinating for negative reasons: Talk with others you trust to determine how to end this pattern.

ORGANIZING YOUR LIFE FOR SCHOOL

Throughout this book, we've emphasized making your Basic Choice in the most favorable way possible. Sometimes, the best opportunity lies in going to school (full- or part-time) and positioning yourself better for the future.

If you are in school, or plan to go to school to improve your prospects, you can and should treat this opportunity like a job. Whether you pursue education in day school, night school, or summer school, the basic procedure is the same. Focus on your objectives. Thoroughly prepare for every test of your knowledge, skills, and abilities. Present yourself in the best possible light.

You should also evaluate your options and select the best route open to you. Once you have chosen your school, continue by selecting the best courses available to you in that school. Clear away other parts of your daily schedule so you can give your schooling enough time and energy. And—perhaps most important—follow through until you reach your goal.

There are many levels of schooling you can pursue, depending on how far you have come and what goals you are trying to achieve. There are too many options and possibilities to discuss here in any meaningful detail. However, you can easily find plenty of useful information. Start in your local library by looking through school catalogs. Discuss your objectives with a good reference librarian and you may find a great deal of information on the opportunities open to you. But even if you find only the names of several schools to which you might apply, there are almost certainly guidance counselors and admissions counselors at those schools who can help you make the best possible choice.

You may have other resources available to you, too. People in the field you are trying to pursue may be able to describe the level of schooling you need and steer you toward the available options. You may also have family members who know of good schools you could attend.

Chapter 11 contains a plan for everyone who has a mission or a dream. Let your mission or dream be to gain more schooling, and use this plan to help you follow through on your educational opportunities. Getting a better education can be difficult, expensive, and time-consuming, but all of this is more in the nature of an investment than an expense. Not only will your extra education help you get more enjoyment and satisfaction out of life, but it will probably help increase your earnings and thus pay you back for the time and trouble you've spent in going to school.

ORGANIZING YOUR LIFE FOR A SECOND INCOME

For many hardworking people, incomes in recent years have failed to keep pace with the rising cost of living, and the idea of developing a second income has started to look better and better.

There's nothing wrong with taking a second job or running a sideline business to earn extra money. The main problem for most people who try is that they fail to take advantage of the organizing principles, strategies, and techniques we've discussed elsewhere in this book. They work hard, but they make poor Basic Choices. Ultimately, they fail to apply themselves to their most important objectives. As a result, they burn themselves out, compromise their health, jeopardize their relationships and other important areas of their lives. But earning a second income does not have to cost more than it's worth.

Basically, organizing your life to earn a second income without killing yourself or the quality of your life requires you to put a simple plan into effect: First, tighten up your existing responsibilities; second, identify your best opportunities; and third, work at the best available option.

Tighten Up Your Existing Responsibilities

Few people who want to earn a second income have four to eight hours a day of relatively unused time. If you want to work more, you'll have to take time from other activities. So the first logical step is to consolidate and compress your important activities to free up as much extra time as possible. This way, you'll probably still have time for most of what is important to you, even though you're working two jobs.

If you've been going through the Experiences in this book and applying what you've learned to your daily life, you've already done a good deal of compression and paring away of your lowest-priority items. To accomplish still more, get into a "hurry up" mode from time to time.

To understand this mode, consider the situation where a routine task you're trying to do takes half a day. Then one day you're facing an extraordinary emergency and you find a way to get the task done in two hours. That's the "hurry up" mode in action. Shaving big chunks of time from a task this way often requires you to:

- Lower your standards and accept less accuracy
- Get help from others
- Combine tasks
- Utilize existing or ready-made components
- Make use of new tools or techniques
- Move faster

For example, suppose you are responsible for drawing a chart for a weekly presentation. You normally spend an hour preparing the information and drawing the chart, but one day you find you have just thirty minutes before you're expected to deliver this week's chart. You may decide to use last week's chart and simply replace the numbers that have changed. You may discover that a nearby art-supply house has ready-made graph paper of the right size, which can help you draw the lines for your chart far faster and easier. You may enlist an assistant or colleague to do some of the basic chart work while you calculate this week's numbers. You may even invent a new format for the chart that makes the presentation clearer—and easier to draw. You'll certainly cut down on wasted motion and move a good deal faster than you normally do. However you do it, there's a good chance you'll finish this week's chart in the available time.

The hidden advantage of the "hurry up" mode is that, once you use it to accomplish a task in a much shorter time, you can keep doing the task this way even when you're not in a hurry. You've instantly freed a good deal of extra time for other work.

Under pressure to earn a second income, you'll want to start cutting back on less important activities and the time you spend on lower priorities. Combine activities—for example, spend time with several friends at once or wash the dishes while you watch your favorite TV show. Focus on your family, friends, and top responsibilities. Concentrate more, so you get maximum pleasure and benefit from the time you spend on your top-priority items.

Identify Your Best Opportunities

Finding a second job is more than a matter of glancing through the want ads. You'll want to earn the maximum income for the minimum number of hours. To do this, you'll want to focus on your strengths, then put them to work in an area where they'll win the most appreciation and rewards.

If you're happy in your present work, the simplest idea is either to do more of it or to find another job just like it. But this may be difficult. For example, if you're selling real estate, you may not be able to sell any more than you already do. But this approach can work for many other people. For example, a dental hygienist I know was able to increase her income by taking a second job, part-time, in another dental office. Similarly, a landscaper found a second job working Saturdays for a different company in the same business.

Some jobs don't lend themselves to duplication but can nevertheless provide a basis for finding related work. For example, a machinist in the Midwest couldn't find a second skilled job in her city, so she signed on to do some inventory management at a nearby specialty metals supplier. Her knowledge of the materials made her well qualified for this work. Similarly, a grade school teacher couldn't get more teaching work, but he was able to find part-time employment with a textbook publishing company.

To pursue this idea, identify your employment strengths. Start by listing the skills and experience you have now. Then consider their implications. What other work might you be able to do, or learn to do, because of what you already know?

Once you have an idea of what you can offer, start developing a list of likely employers in your area. Use the Yellow Pages or local lists of industry. One of the local libraries will probably have Yellow Pages from all the surrounding towns, plus other listings you can consult.

Use the time you've freed up from your personal life to make contact with all these potential employers, at least a few of them every day. Ask the person in charge of personnel or hiring about any existing opportunities. If appropriate, make a pitch about your own strengths and experience. Ask if new opportunities will be opening in the future, and call back from time to time to keep in touch with each firm's evolving employment picture.

Work at the Best Available Option

Assuming you've identified your strengths, zeroed in on likely employers, and kept in contact with them, at some point you'll be offered a job. If after six months only one job turns up, you'll probably want to snap at it. But if you're offered several different opportunities within a short period of time, you'll want to evaluate them and select the best.

Of course, you'll have to make your own judgment about which opportunity to accept. But in making your judgment, you can follow the basics we've been covering in this book. Define your objectives. Consider how well each of the opportunities might help you reach them. Balance what you must give up for each opportunity against what you expect to gain.

Run a Sideline Business

One opportunity that probably won't be offered to you, but which may make the most sense, is to run a sideline business. Of course, you may not have skills that will work in an independent business. But most jobs today, from janitor to marketing vice president, can be reorganized into a business and offered under contract to organizations that would normally hire a full- or part-time employee to do the very same work. Thousands of people without special training or advanced degrees have made a success of such a sideline business.

For example, a woman who once worked full-time for hospitals as a specialist in developing new programs has recently opened a consulting business where she does exactly the same work for a great deal more money. Similarly, an accountant supplements the income from his full-time job by performing audits and doing monthly financial work for small companies in his area. An illustrator with a job at an advertising agency takes freelance assignments to generate additional money. Several women I know are paid to go shopping in supermarkets; they check the accuracy of prices and the quality of products, then make written reports to the supermarket company's management. A secretary supplements her income by doing medical transcription for several doctors in her town. An out-of-work artist has built a business making custom stained-glass windows that he gets decorators to sell to their clients. There are countless other possibilities.

Once you zero in on some ideas that intrigue and excite you, do a little research. Business libraries have information on starting and planning a venture, including sample business plans and case histories of entrepreneurs who have succeeded in particular lines. Publishing companies sell books on sideline businesses, and magazines devoted to your selected industry may run occasional articles on start-up successes or failures, either one of which will help you identify what it takes to succeed and what problems you're likely to encounter.

Before you invest too much time or money in starting a sideline business, be sure to work up a business plan that addresses the twin keys to success:

a) Generating a steady flow of business
b) Setting your prices at profitable levels

If you hope to generate a good income in the first few days of your venture, forget the sideline business and look for a second job instead. A sideline business requires staying power, usually based on a steady income from well-established sources. However, if you can keep the sideline business operating for six months or a year, it can prove a great way to substantially increase your income, your productivity, and your success.

CHAPTER 5

BASIC PRINCIPLES
OF EFFECTIVENESS

I pointed out earlier in this book how increasing your effectiveness requires an effort something akin to the scientific method. As with the scientific method, you begin with a series of general operating principles, which you apply to every situation.

Efforts to accomplish more of what you want require a two-tiered discipline:

a) On the *first tier* are literally hundreds of specific techniques for doing more in less time, eliminating tedious chores, speeding communications, and erasing other problems. (You saw most of these in Chapter 4.)

b) On the *second tier* are a few basic principles that come together in varying combinations to generate those specific techniques. These principles, in fact, are often applications of basic patterns that work successfully elsewhere. Not surprisingly, what improves efficiency and productivity in one area of your work and your life often does the same in other areas, too.

Until now, we've concentrated on specific techniques to improve your effectiveness and accomplish more of what you want. This is because the general principles are often considered too abstract, too difficult to apply without firsthand experience of them in action. Now that you've looked at your goals, studied how you spend your time, and concentrated on improving your productivity, you can take a step back and consider the basic principles governing all your efforts so far.

In this chapter, we concentrate on these basic principles. Armed with these proven patterns of success, you can literally devise new techniques to carry you through whatever unique chores, complications, or problems you may face. It's important at this time to learn the principles for another reason: Without them, you can go no further than to memorize specific techniques—and to hope you use the right one at the right time. With an understanding of success-oriented principles, however, your ability to accomplish what you want is unlimited. Your memory and your creativity give you a one-two punch that can knock out most or all of the obstacles blocking further increases in your level of effectiveness and success.

One caution, however. Don't be alarmed if some of these principles seem to set a pretty stiff standard of behavior. They present an idealized standard, not a rigid requirement. Because they are principles, not examples, I state them at full strength. But no one expects perfection. Since the principles are going to serve as beacons, I prefer to let them shine out brightly. But don't let them blind you to the value of improved performance, even if you cannot fully meet the standard.

Now let's go over these principles one by one.

ESTABLISH GOALS

This is an absolute basic that we have already covered elsewhere in this book. I include it here only as a reminder of its importance and to provide a complete picture of the basic principles.

In essence, this principle tells you to start every day, every action, every project with a firm notion of specific accomplishments that will satisfy you. For clarity, each of your goals should include the following:

a) A description of the accomplishment you desire.
b) An objective method of measuring your progress toward this accomplishment, together with criteria, so that you or anyone else can easily determine whether or not you achieve your goal.
c) A reasonable deadline or general time frame for making progress toward this accomplishment. This is useful as an aid in making your Basic Choice and ensuring that your goal does not lie unused and unattained for too long.

In practice, the objective method and specific criteria you establish for measuring your progress will be extremely helpful as tools for determining what you really want. This is because to articulate this method and these criteria, you must first understand your goal in detail. And the more you know about a particular goal, the more you know whether or not it is one you'd like to accomplish.

WORK DIRECTLY TOWARD YOUR GOALS

This principle is the foundation for setting priorities, and it meshes well with the principle of Finish First Things First (see page 165). The idea behind this principle is simple: Having established what accomplishment will satisfy you, it is only logical to realize that you can gain a greater level of satisfaction by accomplishing more of your goals. And trying to do this leads you to:

a) Put as much time and effort as possible into working toward your goals. You should avoid spending time or energy on activities that do not lead you toward them.
b) Simplify and eliminate side issues and niceties if they hobble or detour you.
c) Return to working toward your goal(s) immediately after any and all detours.

You may want to think of yourself as a homing pigeon. Despite the distance, the obstructions, and the dangers, you always turn toward home. Why? Because heading directly for home presents the straightest course from your present position to the place you want to be.

Not surprisingly, persistence and perseverance are important elements in your long-range effort to accomplish the results you want.

WORK TO A FIRM DEADLINE

A deadline was once a line on a military prison floor. If the prisoners crossed it, they were shot. Today a deadline is a less dangerous time limit, but it retains almost the same ability to command your attention and force your compliance. Deadlines have immense power to make you more effective. A deadline—whether you aim it at others or yourself—helps even a weak suggestion get action. In addition, a deadline gives meaning to your activities, provides one basis for measuring your accomplishments, and helps you focus on and make each of your Basic Choices.

You have probably noticed how you work faster and more effectively when you try to meet an important deadline. You can provide yourself the same benefits if you set and try to meet deadlines on all your projects. Even when you have a deadline set by someone else, you can add to its value by setting your own a few days earlier. If you supervise other people, you can help them improve their performance on any task by helping them to recognize and meet appropriate deadlines. And you get these results almost automatically.

How often have you asked someone for a favor and had your request amiably shelved? You say something like, "Fred, would you bring back my garden hose, please? I need to wash down the back fence with it." Fred will say, "Sure." But he probably won't bring you the hose. Without a deadline, your request was just another line in the conversation, as quickly forgotten as an offhand comment about the weather.

Now look what happens when you add a simple deadline: "Fred, would you bring back my garden hose, please? I need to wash down the back fence with it by Friday." The whole character of your request is different. Fred immediately begins thinking about how long it has been since he borrowed your garden hose, about whether he will need it after Friday, about how he can possibly get it to you by Friday, even about why you might need it by Friday and not Saturday. Your deadline gives life to your request, makes it more urgent, and opens a good deal wider the door to getting it answered.

A deadline works the same magic on the job. You ask a supplier for a delivery of rubber bands, for example, and he says, "Sure." But you don't get them for a week and a half, maybe a month and a half! If you add a deadline to your request, you'll get a much better response.

You can drop a deadline on yourself, too. In fact, you absolutely must give yourself deadlines if you expect to tackle those projects in the back of your mind, the ones that will take you toward your lifelong goals. Fact the facts: You have been aware of some of these goals for a long while. And you are intelligent and practical enough to know some of the steps you must take to accomplish them. But you haven't done much about them. Why? Because there was no deadline pushing you toward action.

Without a deadline for your important goals, urgent items automatically seem more important. Like millions of other people, you neglect your truly important tasks at least partly because you never set a time by which to complete them. Use Experience 16 to set some deadlines for yourself today. You'll soon see the difference they make.

Experience 16

Self-Evaluation: Five Deadlines to Meet

Instructions: The object here is to establish for yourself at least five key deadlines for five projects that are important to you. The sooner you begin to set some deadlines and make the personal determination to beat them, the sooner you can get the power of the deadline principle working for you.

1) In your personal notebook, list at least five important projects or activities you have been wanting to accomplish for a month or longer but have found no time to work on.

2) For each one, list the major steps you must complete to achieve your goal.

3) For each project or activity, estimate from your own expe-

rience (or just guess) how many days must elapse between starting and finishing each step. Add up all the days for each project or activity.

4) Use the total elapsed time you estimate you need for each activity to calculate a reasonable deadline for you to complete it. Take into account the order in which you want to tackle the five projects or activities, as well as your ability to work on several simultaneously. Write down your deadline next to each project or activity on your list.

You'll probably notice that the work you do to meet a deadline takes on extra meaning. It's one thing to paint your house yourself; it's another to finish in time for the family gathering in June! It's nice to cook a delicious gourmet meal; it's even more meaningful to get it on the table by eight-thirty, when your guests are ready to eat. You naturally set most deadlines according to when you need or want the results. Therefore, meeting your deadline satisfies you twice: once by bringing you the basic results, and again by giving you the satisfaction of getting those results when you want them. You may even find a third satisfaction: the good feeling you get just from meeting a self-imposed deadline. All of this contributes to the meaning and enjoyment you find in accomplishing a specific task.

Deadlines also provide a convenient and objective method of measuring your accomplishments. It might be hard to calculate how well you're doing your job. But it's very easy to count up the number of deadlines you meet, the number you miss, and compare. It's also easy to calculate the "time overrun" for each deadline you miss—both the number of days you overran your deadline and the percentage of overrun on the entire project. Over the long term, deadlines provide a good basis for measuring your effectiveness.

At home, it's fairly difficult to check your progress on many or most of your projects. But a deadline makes this easier. Give yourself specific deadlines for meeting specific objectives. Then count up how many of your deadlines you meet and how many you miss. But don't be rigid about this: Give yourself humane and reasonable goals. Your diet? Give yourself some deadlines for reaching specific weights. Your social life? Give yourself some deadlines for meeting a specific number of new people. Give yourself more deadlines—for getting out of the house, seeing new movies, joining new clubs, finding new partners, or whatever you enjoy. Physical fitness? Give yourself a deadline for getting in reasonable enough shape to jog a good distance, and another, longer deadline for going that distance at a fast pace. Whatever you do, whatever you want to do, you can measure your performance (and make it more meaningful) if you set deadlines and try to meet them.

Finally, a deadline is a useful criterion when you make your Basic Choice of "What to do next." Faced with a bewildering list of options and a confusing array of rewards, penalties, preparedness, and desire, you can often simplify your Basic Choice by considering deadlines. If everything else is equal, or too confusing to cope with, you may decide to give your first attention to the item with the least time to spare before its deadline comes due. For example, suppose you must straighten the house for a party, clean the pool, do the marketing, and watch the NBA Finals on TV. You have until 6 P.M., when the market closes, to go shopping; until 8 P.M., when your guests arrive, to finish the straightening; until 8:30 or 9 P.M., when people will want to use your pool, to clean it; and the Finals are on TV right now, noon. Isn't it obvious? Watch the game now, then rush out to do the marketing (can you do this during haltime?), then straighten up the house, and clean the pool in whatever time is left over. Deadlines help organize your day!

How to use a Deadline

All you must do to harness the power of deadlines is to respect them when they're given, and to set and respect them when they're not. Set reasonable deadlines: far enough ahead so you can do the task without unnecessary rushing, but close enough so you have little time to spare for delays. Choose your deadlines from among the following four types:

Type 1: Ordered by someone else, but negotiable. A moderately strong prompt, depending on just how "negotiable" it turns out to be. Some demands are easily turned aside; others require massive trade-offs for the smallest bit of flexibility.

Type 2: Ordered by someone else and not negotiable. An extremely strong prompt, with equally strong consequences for failure. If the train leaves at 3 P.M., either you're on it or you're not.

Type 3: Built into the task. A very strong, often imperative time limit, such as when cooking four-minute eggs or when free-diving underwater. Physical laws and personal capabilities predominate here.

Type 4: Added on to the task. A very strong prompt. Usually created by chronologically juxtaposing two separate tasks, such as having to return a rented car by noon and also having to drop off your mother at her sister's house; or trying to become a millionaire by age thirty-five.

SCHEDULE IN REVERSE

As a basic principle, this guideline has wide application. The key idea is to look first at where you want to end up, then:

a) Analyze the work so you know how much time each step or phase will require

b) Schedule each step or phase in reverse order so you know the Latest Feasible Starting Date you can safely use to meet your deadline

Let's see how this principle works in practice to complete, for example, a report by the fifteenth of the month. First, we use our experience and judgment to chop the task into short, manageable steps. Second, we start on the deadline date and allow time for each step, calculating backward. For this report, our steps (in reverse order) might include: final-draft typing and proofreading (one day), final-draft writing and correcting (two days), rough typing (one day), rough-draft writing and correcting (three days), thinking and planning report (three days), gathering materials (three days).

It looks as though we need about thirteen working days to complete this report. By scheduling in reverse from the deadline, we find our Latest Feasible Starting Date to be thirteen working days before the fifteenth, or the twenty-seventh of the previous month. This calculation also gives us target starting and ending dates for each step of the project.

Any way you plot a project's steps on your calendar, you're ahead of the game. But scheduling in reverse is more effective than scheduling forward because you get a more accurate picture of how to meet your deadline. If you naively schedule a given Project A from today forward, you can make mistakes. For example:

a) You may neglect or delay other current valuable work because you are working too long or too hard on Project A. Better way: Schedule Project A in reverse, then delay or reduce your involvement in Project A as much as possible—until you finish project due sooner.

b) You may rush to finish Project A too fast, then find yourself stuck with little or no other work to do. Better way: Schedule Project A in reverse, then work just enough on Project A to keep it moving along while you simultaneously look for other projects and opportunities to do now before they evaporate from neglect. If you haven't analyzed Project A and you're unsure of how long you need to complete it, you may miss out unnecessarily on all your other possibilities.

c) You may finish Project A, then discover new information or learn a new trick that forces you to redo some or all of your work. Better way: Schedule Project A in reverse, then delay Project A until your Latest Feasible Starting Date. This way, you can bring to bear on Project A all your experience and the latest available information.

MATCH YOUR WORK TO YOUR CAPACITIES

This principle dictates that, ideally, you should try to:

a) Recognize the moment-by-moment variations and changes in your capacity to do work

b) Select work that just matches your capacity of the moment

The advantage of following this principle is significant: You are most effective when you are working at or near your full capacity. When you take on a task that's too easy, you are for the moment underemployed.When you try to handle one that's too hard, you are for the moment overemployed. Either way, you're less effective than when at your best. So the more consistently you match your work to your capacities, the more effective you'll be overall.

But don't be fooled. The simplicity of this idea doesn't make it easy to follow. You need practice to recognize your own capacity for work at a given moment. And you need a different kind of practice to start making your Basic Choice at least partly on the basis of your current capacity to meet a task's demands. Let's look a little deeper into how you can put this principle to use.

Recognize Your Capacity

You've probably heard of many "cycles" that affect people. And you probably recognize that there are cycles within cycles within cycles. For example, there are: astrological cycles from less than a minute to thousands of years in length; lifelong cycles of development and decline; annual cycles, seasonal cycles; biorhythmic cycles lasting several weeks; daily cycles of sleeping and waking, of full alertness and lethargy; and many more. Dr. Dorothy Tennov at the University of Bridgeport has reportedly discovered body cycles that influence our performance minute by minute!

Your capacity for work at any given moment is the sum of all these cycles. It's a tough trick to figure your capacity for work without a computer. But you can make your guesses far more accurate with practice. Start by looking for cycles in your Time Log (explained in Appendix A). For example, try to find a pattern in your work on high-, medium-, and low-capacity tasks.

Pay attention to your feelings while you work, too. Begin to check yourself more frequently to see how you rate (1 is the lowest, 10 the highest) on each of the five "dimensions" of your capacity to work (see Experience 17 and accompanying chart). These five dimensions come together in various ways to influence your effectiveness at any given moment.

Use Experience 17 to map your personal ups and downs on the five key dimensions. As you practice monitoring your capacities, you will soon improve your ability to recognize your capacity fluctuations.

Once you have filled in Experience 17 a few times, look at your high-, medium-, and low-capacity efforts to see if they form a daily, weekly, or longer pattern. If they show one, then you have a strong clue to your capacity for work at any moment.

Your capacities not only shrink and grow, they lean and sway like a growing plant: first in one direction, then in another, as a part of you that is vigorous and strong predominates, then another part takes over. And these cycles occur from year to year, day to day, hour to hour, even minute to minute in some instances. The story "Flowers for Algernon," made into the film *Charly,* with Cliff Robertson, was the exaggerated tale of a man who cycles from subnormal intelligence to superintelligence and back within a few months. If you observe children, you may notice that a child who is vigorous, attentive, and smart as a whip one moment can be tired, cranky, and maddeningly slow the next. Children's capacities vary much more rapidly than ours, but in the same general way. Our capacities cycle slowly enough that we can usually finish what we start. But if you're trying to maximize your effectiveness, don't leave this to chance.

Experience 17

Five Dimensions of Your Work Capacity

Instructions: In your personal notebook, rate your capacity to work at this moment. List the date and time. Then give yourself a rating of 1 (lowest) to 10 (highest) on each of the following dimensions. Review this rating sheet later for analysis and comparison.

1) Feeling strong, tireless
2) Feeling smart, creative
3) Feeling courageous, like a leader
4) Feeling talkative, persuasive
5) Feeling warm toward others, understanding

Essential Capacities for Work

Feeling:	Best Suited For:
Strong, tireless	• Handling paperwork • Starting new projects • Doing lengthy or boring tasks
Smart, creative	• Solving problems • Developing new opportunities • Meeting challenges
Courageous, like a leader	• Attending meetings • Making committee decisions • Initiating projects
Talkative, persuasive	• Handling negotiations • Making personal contacts • Building support for your agenda
Warm toward others, understanding	• Evaluating of others • Advising others • Seeking advice

Be attentive to how you feel at various moments of the day and the week. Try to discern a pattern of highs and lows, strengths and weaknesses. Many people feel stronger during the morning or during the earlier part of the week. Others find extra strength toward the end of the day or week. Some personal patterns are more subtle than this. Try to take advantage of your strength and compensate for your weaknesses as you notice your capacities fluctuate.

Use All Your Capacity

Once you can size up your capacity of the moment, try to select the one task that suits you best. For example, if you are feeling tired and not too alert, don't start working on your tax return. You'd be tackling a task far above your capacity, and you'd drown in that sea of paperwork like a poor swimmer in a riptide. It would be a better choice to go over a draft of a letter or report; it's a job you're more familiar with and one that's less demanding than taxes. Wait until you're feeling tireless and smart to do your tax return.

On the other hand, it's not a very good idea to go over that letter when you're feeling courageous and talkative. You'd want to rewrite it in a whole new way. This is the time—if you're ever going to do it—to climb the north face of Mount Everest or start negotiating with your boss for that long overdue raise!

Selecting a task to match your immediate capacities is a straightforward process:

a) Determine your current capacities—in terms of a numerical self-score on each of the five dimensions listed in Experience 17. With practice, this will take about fifteen seconds.

b) Look over your list of tasks and start making your Basic Choice of what to do next.

c) Determine the capacity demands of the task you have in mind. Give it a numerical score on each of the same five dimensions. With practice, this will take about twenty seconds.

d) If your score is within 2 points of the task's score on all dimensions, consider that task okay right now. If the discrepancy is more than 2 points on any dimension, it's not a good match. Try to select a better one. In practice, take the task that most closely matches your capacities of the moment.

e) Take on a task that's a terrible match in only two critical situations: 1) important reasons make the task vital to do right away; and/or 2) you have no better alternative.

CONCENTRATION

Concentration is a basic principle of top-level achievement. It's also a general guideline that saves you time and makes you more effective in a wide variety of situations.

As a basic principle, concentration led to the development of the assembly line, where workers concentrate their skills and attention on performing a few tasks as rapidly and effectively as possible. It's a great idea. Unfortunately, many assembly lines generate some undesirable side effects when they require too much concentration on too dull and repetitive a task. But those drawbacks are easily avoided.

Concentration is also in evidence in most military campaigns. The winner is often the one who "gets there firstest with the mostest." Concentration is the operative principle in effective football plays, weightlifting regimens, laser beams, and ESP demonstrations. Nearly everywhere you turn, in fact, concentration is a powerful technique used to "soup up" effectiveness the way a turbocharger (which concentrates air) boosts the power of an engine.

Intensive Time—the Most Useful

If you review your Time Logs, or just think back on your own experience, you'll probably see you have been most productive and most effective during periods when you were concentrating deeply. To make the best of your natural abilities, learn to maximize your periods of concentration and to set up your environment so you can concentrate for as long as possible:

a) Set aside time when you know you will not be interrupted. A good way to do this is simply to note your least interrupted times of the day and week, then get in the habit of using that time for concentrated work.

b) Prepare the people around you. Get them to respect your periods of concentration. Schedule Quiet Hours (see below), during which you put up a sign or otherwise signal that you wish to concentrate without being distracted or disturbed.

c) Prepare your tasks so you can concentrate without interrupting yourself. Do all the preparatory work. Have all the reference materials and background information at hand. Familiarize yourself with your objectives so you know exactly what you are trying to achieve. Then, when you begin to concentrate, you won't need to break your concentration to handle basic business.

d) Prepare your work space. Sometimes, it is impossible to

concentrate in a familiar environment littered with a million distractions. Sometimes, it is impossible to concentrate unless you *are* in familiar surroundings. Try different places for concentration and see which ones you like best. You may even want to select different locations for different tasks. The key is to find a place where you can concentrate. Once you find one, use it as often as you can.

Quiet Hours for Concentration

Basically a device to augment your self-control, the Quiet Hours has "formal" time limits and specific rules for behavior that help you feel special about it. They also make you feel better about enlisting others' cooperation. The result is to make every minute of the set-aside period count for more concentration, efforts, and results.

Chapter 8 gives you some tips on installing a Quiet Hour to increase your effectiveness.

How to Concentrate

Because your deep-concentration time is so useful, you can boost your effectiveness if you learn to concentrate at will for long periods. Once you know how to reach and maintain a state of concentration, you can apply yourself when and where you wish. Experience 18 gives you a program for boosting your concentration time; this program really works. You can use it to lengthen dramatically the amount of time you are able to concentrate without a break. The basics of the program are these:

a) Measure your current concentration ability.
b) Practice concentrating as long and as hard as you can.
c) Reward yourself for any improvement in your concentration ability, irrespective of the results your concentration brings.

With practice, you can double or triple the length of time you are able to concentrate, and this translates directly into a tremendous boost to your effectiveness. Concentration in regard to your goals and achievements has four main variations:

a) Concentrating (and stretching) your *attention* so you are deeply involved with the task at hand
b) Concentrating your *tasks* so you work in a relatively long burst on many similar or linked tasks
c) Concentrating your *time* by saving minutes here and there and shifting them around to make a block of time
d) Concentrating your *effort* so you accomplish a single purpose despite a number of demands and opportunities

Let's "concentrate" on these variations, one by one:

CONCENTRATING AND STRETCHING YOUR ATTENTION

You probably know how to do this without being told. I would bet you're concentrating your attention right now on "Concentrating Your Attention." This variety of concentration is widely used in a great many businesses and home-life applications. Think for a moment of the familiar comparison: How fast time passes when you're kissing someone you love; how slowly when you're holding your hand over a candle. But notice whichever one you're doing, you're concentrating your attention on it.

Most of us can concentrate. Studying, learning to drive, listening to an interesting story all require concentration of attention. But few of us have ever taken the trouble to practice the art of concentration and thus, by conscious design, build up our ability to concentrate. When you practice your concentration, you gain tremendous benefits:

a) You can concentrate for longer periods, up from the normal thirty minutes or an hour to as much as three hours of intense concentration at a stretch!
b) You can concentrate in less than optimal situations: noisy, drafty, uncomfortable locations, for example; or under conditions of stress, deadline pressure, and/or illness.
c) You can dive into a deep state of concentration much faster, or stop concentrating for a moment, then get right back into it.

You can stretch your ability to concentrate simply by practicing. Here's how: Place a task in front of you. Note the time, then start to concentrate your attention on the task. As soon as you lift your concentration, note the time again. Do this for several repetitions and you'll see a pattern, a limit to how long you can concentrate. To expand this limit, strive to go longer and longer without breaking your concentration. Set goals, and then give yourself rewards for attaining them.

As you practice, notice two things. First, notice that the length of time you can concentrate depends partly on the object of your attention. For example, you can concentrate far longer on something in which you have an avid interest than on something you find boring. To make a useful study of your ability to concentrate, do a Time Log (from Appendix A) as you concentrate on various tasks. Second, notice that when you stretch your ability to concentrate on one task, you can concentrate longer right across the board. This means you can practice concentrating your attention on just about anything, and know that you are automatically improving your power to concentrate for long periods on all your responsibilities. You can develop a self-discipline program designed to stretch your ability to concentrate by following Experience 18.

Experience 18

Building Your Power to Concentrate

Instructions: Keep track of your concentration on at least five different tasks to measure how long you normally concentrate without a break. Consider this your Base Period. From then on:

1) Whenever you settle down to concentrate, note the time. Later, note the time when you feel your concentration dissipate. This constitutes one Concentration Session.

2) If you haven't concentrated long enough to satisfy yourself, do not award yourself a work break just yet. Instead, immediately try to start concentrating again. If you can regain a deep level of concentration, continue working. If you cannot begin concentrating again within three to five minutes, consider this Concentration Session to be over.

3) String together many Concentration Sessions into as long
    a work session as you can without taking a break. When
    you finally stop concentrating on the task, note the full
    length of time you held your concentration. Take your
    work break; you've earned it. But leave your work area
    while on your break.

4) Calculate how many "points" you earned in the work ses-
    sion according to the following table:

    Concentrating during one Base Period earns 1 point
    Concentrating during two Base Periods without a break
        earns 3 points (1 + 2)
    Concentrating during three Base Periods without a break
        earns 7 points (1 + 2 + 4)

If you learn to concentrate longer, double the points you earn
    for each additional Base Period of concentration without a
    break. In my case, before I began this program I could
    concentrate for an hour at a time. So for my first hour of
    unbroken concentration I earned only 1 point. But when
    I learned to concentrate for two hours at a time, I earned
    twice as much, or 2 points for that second hour—3 points
    total for the two-hour work session. When I learned to
    concentrate for three hours at a time, I earned 4 points
    for that third hour, accumulating 7 points during my
    three-hour work session. When I could put in four hours
    without a break, I earned 15 points in a morning's work.

5) Use the points you earn through longer and longer pe-
    riods of concentration to "buy" the right to do something
    you enjoy.

The specific reward you choose is not as important as: a) scor-
    ing yourself honestly, and b) choosing a reward you want
    very much. Given that, the process works almost by itself.

CONCENTRATING YOUR TASKS

This is a great way to get more done faster. For example, if you
return a good many phone calls, you can do each of them more
quickly and effectively by saving up all your calls and making them

in sequence. You tend to get into a rhythm, to erase a lot of uncertainty about what to do next. As a result, you make each call faster and move on to the next one more rapidly.

You can get the same boost in effectiveness no matter what tasks you bunch together, from personal visits to letter writing, opening mail, or stuffing envelopes.

And this is a fairly easy idea to translate into action:

a) *Defer* every task until you are up against deadline pressure.
b) *Organize* these deferred tasks into similar or related groups you can work on in sequence.

CONCENTRATING YOUR TIME

Because periods when you concentrate your attention are your most productive, and efficiency improves as concentration increases, it pays to work in one- to three-hour blocks rather than five- to ten-minute units. But despite our desire and ability to concentrate, most of us must deal with dozens of distractions. In fact, if you are an executive, you probably average over sixty interruptions a day: one every eight to ten minutes. So unless you're very lucky, you usually won't find ready-made opportunities to concentrate and work toward your major goals. The next best alternative is to create your own opportunities.

This can be difficult to do because time, unlike money, cannot be saved up easily or moved about. If you have five minutes to spare right now, for example, you can't put them in your pocket to use later on. You can't easily collect five-minute pieces and change them into a one-hour block. If you could, it would be a lot simpler to increase your ability to achieve the results you want. But nevertheless there are some interesting possibilities:

First, although you can't shift around or save up *time*, you can shift around and save up *tasks*. And with the right manipulation of your schedule, you can get almost the same effect as moving blocks of time.

Second, because time marches on at a steady pace, you can quite easily *plan* to make better use of it. And that gives you an edge in your battle to accomplish more of what you want. If you know you will have fifteen minutes of free time at 3 P.M., you can plan to make the best possible use of that time.

Third, the ability to create and make use of one- to three-hour periods is a learned skill. You can practice, and get the benefits of this skill, in almost any situation. Some jobs, like a policeman on foot patrol, present opportunities to work toward a single goal or mission for a full day. Others, like a high school teacher, are more diverse and tightly scheduled, requiring many smaller tasks in the movement toward larger goals and mission statements, which may take a year or longer to achieve. Yet each of these, and most other work and life situations, will yield to the concentration principle to some degree.

The basic approach to "Concentrating Your Time" picks up where "Concentrating Your Tasks" leaves off. Remember what we just learned:

a) *Defer* every task until you are up against deadline pressure.
b) *Organize* these deferred tasks into similar or related groups you can work on in sequence.

Now build on this by doing something more:

c) *Juggle* your schedule to create large time blocks in which you can work on these groups of tasks. To do this: 1) mark time on your calendar for your most important tasks, 2) mark time between these important tasks for your newly created groups of tasks, and 3) follow your schedule to work on these tasks only during the large blocks of time you have just delineated.
d) *Fill the gaps* in your schedule with more of your most important activities.

You get an edge in this process when you find and rely on patterns that take place in time. You probably go through periods when all your frenzied activity is still not enough to get everything done. Then you go through other periods when you can't find enough to keep busy. These patterns exist in daily, weekly, monthly, and annual cycles. You can use them to help you concentrate your time.

Retailers and the clothing industry, for example, typically experience one or more slow seasons on a regular schedule. In your own situation, you may notice Friday afternoons are exceptionally slow. These are ready-made opportunities to create a Quiet Hour, or to concentrate your efforts toward important objectives, and yet feel reasonably confident you won't have to turn away too many people. You can also use this concentrated time to clean up old business, review and revamp procedures, and gear up for the increased activity you know is coming.

While the process of concentrating your time seems a little awkward at first, it becomes more familiar with practice. As you develop your skills and expertise, you'll find it almost second nature to defer, organize, juggle, and fill the gaps with big projects. And you'll be able to apply this basic principle in hundreds of different situations. The four points in this basic approach will help you eliminate the choppy two- to ten-minute items in your schedule, and sweep the ten- to thirty-minute units that occupy most of your day into a solid Concentration Session. This automatically leaves you with relatively large blocks of vacant time to use for your most important projects.

CONCENTRATING YOUR EFFORT

This is the process of sticking to a single goal despite interference and temptation from a dozen different angles. This aspect of the concentration principle tells you to maximize your effectiveness by doing everything you can to achieve one goal rather than trying to spread your effort too thin.

Unless your natural work pattern is to stick to one project steadfastly until you accomplish it, you will have to study the value of concentrating your effort. For example, a basketball coach may have ten or fifteen priority items to think about, such as: being fair about playing time, developing younger players, forging a cooperative team, and setting up next season's schedule, to name just a few. But when the championship draws near, he's most effective by concentrating his effort on winning just the next game. Similarly, you may have half a dozen chores at home to get out of the way, but if you try to do them all at once, you may accomplish nothing. You're more effective concentrating your effort on the most important item until it's done, and then turning your attention to the next one down the line.

Concentrating your effort is not always the best course, of

course. You may be under pressure to distribute your effort among several important projects or tasks. But you can safely concentrate your effort when one task meets the following criteria:

a) The results from accomplishing the task will be more beneficial than those from any other task you're facing.
b) The task is set up so that continuous effort will get it done sooner (unlike tasks that have built-in "process times" that you cannot avoid or compress);
c) Concentrating your effort on this task will not allow some other task to "go critical" or cause additional problems.

FINISH JUST ON TIME

Finish your projects on time! Avoid finishing them early!

If you flip back to "Schedule in Reverse" (see page 150), you'll see references to the Latest Feasible Starting Date for a project. As you become more sophisticated in your achievement efforts, you'll realize this is also the Most Desirable Starting Date.

Finishing too early often means you have neglected other, possibly more important activities. It also means you may later be forced to redo your work in the light of last-minute developments.

What's more, finishing too early may lead to redundant effort, because you may shelve the completed work for a while, then find you must refresh your memory and recheck your work for accuracy before you take it to the next stage.

Perhaps most important, finishing too early provides no benefits, in most cases. No one will ever look at the results of a project and say, "And you finished so early, too!" Hardly anyone will know whether you beat a deadline by one minute, one hour, or one year! And as long as you beat your deadline, you're on schedule. Quality of work is much more memorable than beaten deadlines. So there's no point in risking problems by finishing a project too early.

Thus arises the fine art of cutting it close: starting a project as late as possible but finishing on time. Here's where scheduling in reverse becomes a golden rule, worth its weight in precious hours you can save for better purposes. But note this: We're not talking about unwise delays that later force you to scramble and cut corners to meet your deadline. Leave yourself enough time to do top-quality work. But it's a challenge and a thrill to leave just enough time. Here are some tips that make finishing just on time a breeze:

a) Schedule in reverse, but add 10 percent or more time to your schedule for contingencies at each step in the project.
b) Add another 10 percent to the project overall when you set your Latest Feasible Starting Date.
c) Once you have your dates, follow them as strict guide-lines. Stay on track from the first weeks of the project so you won't be too far behind at the end.
d) Listen to people who claim you're cutting your schedule too tight. This advice is correct more often than not. Allow more leeway for any parts of the project that remain in question.

FINISH FIRST THINGS FIRST

This principle emphasizes the need to establish priorities and stick with them. It almost doesn't matter how you establish these priorities. For example, your "first thing" may be a ten-cent project that's due tomorrow, or one that's worth a fortune ten years down the road. You may choose to finish first a simple chore that takes five minutes, or a complex project that requires hours of planning and preparation.

The principle merely requires you to know which among all your projects is of first importance, then to move that project as far along as you can before you work on any other. The more consistently you do this, the more your results will tend to come from your high-priority projects. And since those results are by definition more desirable than results from lesser-priority projects, you'll instantly become more effective.

To put this principle into action:

a) Keep a current list of all tasks and projects you could work on.
b) Give every project on your list a priority rating.
c) Move projects along toward completion in priority or-

der, going as far as you can with the top-priority project before you move to the second-priority one.

In practice, a current list of all your pending projects could fill a book. It's better to divide this list into three priority groups:

Priority C: "Everything I could work on, but probably won't"

Keep this encyclopedia of opportunities in a closet somewhere. Review it only when you're looking for New Year's Eve resolutions material or when you can't think of any valuable projects on which to work.

Priority B: "Projects and chores I'm going to do"

These fifty or a hundred items deserve to be kept on a list that's somewhat accessible. But don't look at them more than once a day; preferably once a week.

Priority A: "Items I'd better do, because I'll be in the worst trouble if I don't and/or in seventh heaven if I do"

These four or five items are your highest-priority items, culled from the "B" list (above) and kept in your pocket for ready reference all day long.

In practice, you'll find it's not always easy to give your projects and chores a simple priority rating. The ideal way would be to somehow "sense" the correct number, from 1 to 100, based on each project's: a) potential benefit when completed, b) potential loss if ignored, c) urgency or deadline considerations, and/or d) importance or long-range payoff. But since this is impossible, we mortals must suffer along with a practical system:

Step 1:   Go back to your goals and become familiar with them again. (If you're trying to set work priorities

here, use your job description and your work-related aims along with your personal goals.)

Step 2: Try to connect every item on your lists of projects
and chores with one or more of your goals.

Step 3: Determine how long you can safely put off each
item, i.e., its Latest Feasible Due Date.

Step 4: Rank the items according to how many goals they
support and how soon you must begin work on
them.

For example, say you're trying to rank the following chores and
work projects:

• Writing a letter to an irate customer in response to a nasty
letter you received two weeks ago
• Drawing up a plan for moving ahead on a survey of people's opinions, which you would love to have completed
three years ago
• Making plans to fly out of town for the next week to meet
some people who may give you some lucrative business opportunities
• Going next door and asking a crucial favor from someone
you really don't like to deal with

According to the practical system, you might rank them as
follows:

Task Number	Number of Goals Met	Number of Days Until Due	Overall Ranking
1	3	21	#4
2	2	10	#3
3	3	1	#2
4	4	1	#1

The practical system may not give rankings with which you are
comfortable, because it may tell you to work on something that's
scary, challenging, or extremely demanding and uncertain. Nor
may it yield entirely perfect, absolutely accurate rankings. But it
does have the distinct advantage of giving you some reasonable
basis on which to make difficult if not impossible judgments.

CHAPTER 6

LEARNING TO WORK WELL WITH PEOPLE: AN ESSENTIAL INGREDIENT

When you think about effectiveness and achievement as much as you have been doing in this book, you may begin to see them as a talent, a force, an energy—something internal that has little to do with other people. However, this viewpoint is way off target.

Until now, we've concentrated mainly on your individual efforts. And we've taken for granted that the maximum results you can hope for in most situations are simply what you can accomplish on your own. But in most cases, other people bring their special abilities and capacities to a project, just as you do. That is, five people coordinating their work on a single project can add their results together and accomplish more than they could working alone. In most situations, other people are as necessary to your achievements and results as you are, and so your ability to achieve your goals is intimately intertwined with other people's efforts.

To be effective in these situations, you must study a broad range of people-oriented skills and techniques, and explore the broader possibilities for managing other people's work in addition to your own. In effect, you must find ways to add their efforts to yours! To the extent you can do this, you move beyond the limits of individual achievement to a higher level limited only by the talent, knowledge, and applied energy of the people with whom you work.

The range of options and opportunities for coordinating other people's activities with your goals includes:

- Delegating
- Cooperating
- Leveraging
- Consulting
- Controlling

Let's examine each one more fully.

DELEGATING TO THE RIGHT PEOPLE

Used well, delegation is a high art. In rough form, of course, it's a well-known process that lets other people contribute their time directly to your goals. This was covered in Chapter 4. But when you concentrate upon, study, and apply the delegation process with more subtlety, you can transform it from a cut-and-dried management technique to a very personal process we might call "human engineering for results."

The key improvement is the skill and sensitivity with which you delegate. To build your skill, you should concentrate on four important factors: relationship, assessment, motivation, and reinforcement.

Form a Relationship

This technique is basic to more effective use of the delegation process. Yet most people ignore it because it's possible to delegate without building a relationship. This may explain why so many people have so many problems delegating and getting good results.

For example, it's logically possible to avoid building any personal relationships at all with your delegates: You can ignore any personal factors and simply command the use of their skills and abilities on behalf of your goals. It's logically possible, but rarely the most productive way to delegate. Without a solid relationship, most people will do only *what you tell them*, not necessarily *what you want*. You will receive very little interest or attention to detail from your delegates, and you should count yourself lucky if you get any more.

In contrast, consider the value of delegating from the solid basis of a good working relationship. There is a common background here between you and your delegate, a history of good working relations. More than likely, you two know how to communicate well, and you like the idea of working together again. Your delegate probably feels well motivated, confident you'll recognize and reward good effort because you have in the past. Your personal relationship helps your delegate feel more involved and more interested in bringing any project to a successful conclusion. His or her performance on the project usually reflects this.

But developing a good basis for working relationships is a tricky process. You must draw and maintain a fine line between being personal enough and being too personal. There are subtle differences in the way you can and should relate to men and women, or people older and younger than you. You must feel out the situation between you and every individual, and choose a warmly professional style appropriate for each one. Each relationship requires certain unique actions from you. However, there are four basic guidelines that will help you in almost every situation:

a) Be honest, frank, and straightforward as often as you possibly can. Show everyone a solid measure of respect as people and as workers. Devious, dishonest, or manipulative behavior will immediately create suspicion, and it will distort your relationships with the people to whom you delegate. You need not help them to the utmost of your ability if you don't want to. But neither should you cut any throats or stab any backs for your own benefit.

b) Reveal only as much about yourself as you comfortably can, and expect about the same level of response in return. Avoid excessively strong personal ties to your delegates. In general, the best work relationships resemble those between most cousins. Your special link gives you a basis for friendship, but rarely is there enough in common to make you best friends.

c) Give credit to delegates or share yours when you can; take blame from delegates or absorb some of theirs about as often. This policy will put you in solidly with the people on whom you depend.

Assess Others' Strengths

Some people think of delegation only as a forrmal process of getting others to contribute time and effort to their goals. For these people, the particulars of who does the contributing can easily fade into the background. But when you, a dedicated student of organizing for effectiveness, consider delegation as "human engineering for results," you see the need for more careful selection of delegates. You understand that certain delegates are best suited to certain tasks, and the more demanding a particular task, the more skillful and talented your delegate must be.

This makes assessing your delegates' strengths and weaknesses very important. One ideal objective of delegation is to find a great match between the delegate and the demands of the task. In practice, you must often be satisfied with coming close rather than actually hitting the mark. But either way you benefit from a careful appraisal of the people available to you.

You can make that appraisal much the same way you did in Experience 17 (Chapter 5), where you were rating your own work capacity. Matching a delegate to a task is essentially the same process. The main difference is that when you delegate, you're looking at someone other than yourself.

Use Experience 19 to match the demands of a task you want to delegate to the most suitable of the people available to you.

Experience 19

Delegation Planning

Instructions: Use this process to compare the capacities of the people to whom you delegate with the tasks you want to assign.

Try to match each task to the most suitable person available to you. You might want to keep—and frequently update—a written file of your evaluations of other people's capacities, so you can more easily make these comparisons on paper.

1) How much time does this person have available to work on a delegated assignment?
2) How much creative ability does this person bring to a delegated assignment?
3) How much courage and leadership ability does this person bring to a delegated assignment?
4) How much verbal ability and persuasiveness does this person bring to a delegated assignment?
5) How much warmth and personal understanding does this person bring to a delegated assignment?

A second quick way to assess your delegates' strengths and weaknesses is simply to keep track of how well they do the job. Each time you delegate an assignment, start a log on the individual's performance. Add to the log after every briefing or report you receive, at every critical point of the process, and after the wrap-up. Keep these logs on file. Then review them quickly the next time you plan to delegate. They'll help you pinpoint the one person who can do the best job for you.

Motivate as You Delegate

You can be instantly more effective with other people just by adding motivation to delegation. Motivation often makes the difference between so-so performance and exceptional results, between casual mistakes and attention to detail, and between uncertain results and success you can count on.

Here are some guidelines to help you add motivation to your delegation technique:

1) REWARD PEOPLE BEFORE AS WELL AS AFTER GOOD RESULTS

It's helpful to say nice things about a useful report or a job someone does well. On-the-spot compliments or congratulations make your delegate feel the work was well done and appreciated.

It's just as helpful to rekindle good feelings at the start of a project. For example, if I ask an associate to deal with a client for me, I try to mention something similar he or she handled well in the past. It comes out sounding like this: "Remember the Pyro Company you worked with last fall? Well, here's another company in the same position. I'd like you to give them the same kind of treatment."

By replaying your delegate's feelings of success and satisfaction on the previous project, you help set the mood for continued good relations and a successful outcome on the new assignment.

2) USE A MOTIVATING STYLE

Autocratic leaders have a firm style that motivates a great many people (although it alienates others). If you have a naturally motivating personality, you're okay on this score. If not, you can probably learn to provide more motivation by adopting a more participative style. Rather than lead autocratically, you invite people to contribute ideas, direction, and judgment, and their involvement leads them to feel more motivated.

For example, the owner of a midwestern printing company likes to stay in direct control of every phase of his business. He hires people who like to work for a strong boss, and he motivates people basically by smiling or frowning in accordance with how well he feels their work is going.

In contrast, an Oregon apparel manufacturer gives his delegates much more leeway to take charge of their projects. And he is much less judgmental of their work in midstream. Like most participative delegators, he tries to specify the results he wants from a project, as well as the "out of bounds" limits beyond his tolerance. As long as his delegates keep within these bounds, he leaves them free to express their personalities in their decisions, use of authority, and choice of work methods and ideas.

To add motivation when you delegate, analyze your natural style and follow it. Use Experience 20 for your analysis. Whichever attitudes or tendencies feel best to you, be aware of them and play them up or down with different people to make the most of your motivational possibilities.

Self-Evaluation: Delegation Style

Instructions: The following questions are designed to help you analyze your delegation style. Answer them honestly in your personal notebook, and when you are finished, read the comments to gain feedback on your delegation style. You need not share your answers with anyone.

1)   When you confront an assignment you ought to consider delegating, it is most often:

   a)   One you hate to do anyway
   b)   One that is too complex for others to do
   c)   One that is too enjoyable to delegate

2)   When you delegate an item, you like to:

   a)   Spell out exactly how to handle every possible situation
   b)   Forget it and go on to the next item
   c)   Trust your delegate to do his or her best, and to ask for help if needed

3)   Once you decide to delegate, you:

   a)   Collar the first person you see
   b)   Pick your delegate carefully, but outline the project only vaguely and leave him or her unaware of the results you want
   c)   Pick your delegate and explain the project, but expect the delegate to find his or her own resources and contacts without bothering you

4)   At the conclusion of a project you have delegated, you like to:

   a)   Move quickly on to the next item on the agenda
   b)   Go over the project and point out what you would have done differently
   c)   Review the good and bad points of the project, and offer positive and negative criticisms of your delegate's performance.

Analysis of Your Answers

1) a) This may be a valid reason for delegating. Just be sure you don't dump only work without satisfaction onto others you depend on. They will eventually rebel.

   b) This is your ego talking. Complex jobs may be simple to others, or may merely require additional training from you to be properly handled. And such complex jobs can be stimulating, challenging, and motivating to your delegates. You can use delegated work of this type to build a loyal team of competent people.

   c) You are entitled to keep a few enjoyable items for yourself. But these could conceivably crowd out your more important work, and earn you a reputation for delegating only "no win" assignments. As long as you keep these tendencies in check, you are probably okay.

2) a) This is important when introducing people to new responsibilities. However, if you become overly detailed and dictatorial, especially with experienced people, you will demotivate them and obtain poorer results than otherwise.

   b) Here you tend to leave people feeling "abandoned" or "up in the air." Some strongly self-determined people respond well to this treatment. But most people want continuing feedback and comments from you.

   c) This is appreciated by most people, but can backfire with those who cannot bring themselves to ask for help or admit their errors.

3) a) This haphazard approach tends to make people avoid you or stand near you, depending on their ambition and career objectives.

   b) You leave people with an uncertain feeling. Most will scurry for guidelines and objectives—if not from you, then from others.

   c) Such a modus operandi can be debilitating to your delegate, particularly if he or she expends hours to an-

swer a question or solve a problem alone when the
right contact or comment from you could have helped
a great deal. This may also convey the idea you don't
want him or her to succeed.

4) a) Here you may miss a great opportunity to motivate
        your delegates. A few minutes of laudatory talk will
        usually lodge in the mind and heart, and result in bet-
        ter performance at the next opportunity.
   b) You are being insulting at worst, pompous at best.
        Dwelling on "how the old man would have done it"
        and other might-have-beens makes delegates feel they
        can never do well enough to please you. This ap-
        proach motivates very few people to work harder.
   c) This is a useful approach, and worth the few minutes
        it takes. The indirect payoffs more than make up for
        the short lapse from direct action toward your im-
        portant goals.

---

3) SHOW CONFIDENCE IN YOUR DELEGATES

Confidence or lack of confidence is often a self-fulfilling proph-
ecy. In many cases, your delegate will simply live up, or down, to
your expectations. So pick people in whom you have confidence
and show them how you feel. Then let them go to work. You may
feel the best performers can achieve beyond their capacities solely
in order to "prove themselves" to the boss. But this is an American
myth, talked or written about much more often than done.

In the practical world, you rarely get the best results from your
delegates when you openly doubt them and defy them to prove
themselves to you. Instead, you generally get the best results when
you openly and directly show your honest confidence in them. Your
personal style may lead you to demonstrate your confidence with
action or to voice it in words. Either way works, provided you
communicate to your delegates just how deep your confidence
runs.

4) SPREAD THE GOOD WORD ABOUT YOUR DELEGATE

Take your delegate around to other people with whom he or she
will work on the project. Show everyone concerned your good

feelings about the project and your delegate. The more of these positive messages you give, the more you will nurture your delegate and improve your chances of getting good results.

5) "READ" YOUR DELEGATE'S WORRIES AND ASSUAGE THEM

Most delegates have a few worries or concerns about the assignment at the start. Get these out in the open and take care of them.

Ask your delegate directly, "Are you concerned about any part of this project? Do you feel one or two parts of it may be much harder than the rest?" Use the answer to spot any special worries. Then make any changes you can to ease them. If, for example, your delegate is worried about other projects already pending, work out a plan for handling them. If your delegate is having a crisis of confidence, shore him or her up with your own positive expectations and evaluations.

Sometimes, a delegate will have worries he or she won't openly express. Here is where you must "read" his or her face and body language for tension or discomfort, very often clues to inner worries. By asking questions and noting the nonverbal reaction, you can often come close enough to the concern to guess at the changes you could make to ease the problem. Offer to make those changes. This is just another form of support that, in the long run, will help you get more effectiveness from your delegates.

BUILDING A SYSTEM OF COOPERATION

If you have a lot of work due soon and need help from someone to make sure you can complete it, or you have made a mistake and need a favor in order to correct it without too much loss of time or money, in a very real sense you are asking for cooperation. All of us rely on cooperation from others to do our jobs well, to enjoy our lives, even to survive.

For example, a clerk at a neighborhood dry cleaning store relies on workers in the back room to help him keep his promises to customers. Without their cooperation, he's powerless to offer faster turnaround or special services. Similarly, an editor of a publishing company relies on sales and promotion people to push a book he has fought to publish. Without their cooperation, his acquisitions will fall flat in the bookstores.

Favors like these are most difficult to obtain when you need help from peers or organizational superiors. You have little or no power to compel them to help you, as you do with friends, subordinates, or those you can otherwise influence or control. You must fall back on the goodwill you've accumulated, plus any inherent willingness to cooperate these people may feel. In practice, therefore, getting people to cooperate with you involves constructing a web of relationships.

To double your effectiveness when you look for cooperation, follow these basic guidelines:

a) Keep in touch with people who have helped you before. They are the ones most likely to help you again.

b) Treat people well and leave a trail of goodwill behind you.

c) Don't beat your head against the wall. If someone is aloof or hard to talk to when you need cooperation, look elsewhere. Chances are, he or she would probably say "No" to your request, anyway, or be uncooperative if it came to any actual effort.

Get the Support You Need

You can obtain support from people around you without resorting to the "three B's": brute force, blackmail, or bribery. You can make a positive bid for support from others by following the "ABC's" of purposeful efforts:

Ask for the help you want and need.

Be the first to offer favors so people will feel inclined to help you when you ask.

Create a situation in which helping you lets people help themselves, too. The more directly you can change situations so people benefit when you do, the more support you will get from the people around you.

In general, working well with people entails being pleasant, helpful, honest, and fair. The more often you find ways to apply these basic behaviors in your own situation, the more effectively you will be able to add their achievements to your own.

You can nearly always accomplish more by working with cooperative rather than uncooperative people. Cooperative people show their colors clearly by their friendly disposition, professionalism, and general receptivity to your requests and appeals for help. Not surprisingly, uncooperative people usually "don't have time" to talk to you. They're less friendly, and frequently demand to know what they'll get in return for cooperating. When you must have cooperation from such people, you can use special techniques to apply a little more pressure and build a system of cooperation that's harder for people to resist. So to make sure you get what you want and need effectively, you must use leverage.

USING HUMAN LEVERAGE

Imagine yourself the fulcrum, and your energy and resources the lever. Human leverage is the art of moving close to people on whom you rely and balancing the situation so they benefit from cooperating with you about as much as you benefit from cooperating with them, or even more. This leveraging process turns one-way reliance into a two-way mutual cooperation pact that greatly improves your ability to achieve what you want.

The basic techniques of human relations leverage are simple:

a) Build genuine relationships with the people on whom you rely.
b) Use your power, influence, and resources to make their life easier or more satisfying—make them indebted to you.
c) Try to balance your reliance on them with their reliance on you. The more difficult it would be for you to get along without them, the more indispensable to them you should try to become.

"Qualify" Your Contact

Working closely with others is a proven method for getting your work accomplished, particularly when you need their agreement or cooperation. But you can be much more effective in working with others if you make sure to work with the right person.

The most common instance of depending on others may be when a salesman asks for an order. But it's worthless to ask for an order from a person who doesn't have the authority to say "Yes." To avoid this problem, the most successful salespeople try to "qualify" a prospect right away. They want to know if the prospect is the key person who must agree to what they want. To find out, effective salespeople will look and listen alertly, and ask pointed questions if necessary.

You can apply this idea to get better results when you work with others toward your goals and responsibilities. Make sure that the other person is qualified to give you the help you need. If not, save your breath for someone who has the knowledge, skills, authority, or time to help you achieve what you want.

CONSULTING WITH OTHERS

This is a great way to identify early those options and plans that have no chance of working. If you're like most people, you can probably fool yourself quite often about the quality of your own ideas. But you'll find it much harder to fool the people around you.

To be most effective, develop and maintain relationships with people whose judgment you trust. These people provide a personal feedback system on which you can rely. Use it! For example, one recent college graduate had the idea of looking for work with a social service agency. She felt a job like this would provide a special opportunity for personal fulfillment and professional growth. But before she accepted the job, she talked with several people she trusted. They described enough realities of social service agency work to change her estimation of the rewards and opportunities she was likely to find. Had she not consulted with her more experienced friends, she would have taken a job that could not possibly have satisfied her particular interests.

As you develop relationships with people whose judgment you trust, begin talking to them about your plans and ideas. Invite them to comment, criticize, and offer opinions. Realize that their comments may not always be on target but that they can help you anyway. In addition to the insights and points of view they offer, talking with them will help *you* spot flaws, problems, and oversights in your thinking. And spotting these rough spots before you take action will invariably make you more effective and improve your results.

CONTROLLING YOUR TIME WITH PEOPLE

If you review the material on interruptions in Chapter 4, you'll find that one key idea is to take control of the time you spend with other people. For example, you take control of your time by refusing to let unimportant interruptions break up your day. You take further control by carefully, conveniently, and effectively scheduling your appointments and meetings.

One basis of such control is to think carefully about who has and should have the right to impose their special expectations on you. As an example, high school or college teachers generally have first call on their students. They not only compel attendance in class, they can cause whole nights and weekends to be devoted to the projects they specify. Students, in contrast, can impose relatively few expectations on their teachers: to show up in class, to grade any work turned in, and perhaps to participate a few times in brief student/teacher conferences. It's much the same situation on the job: Your boss can expect you to be at work for certain regular hours of your day, and sometimes for overtime hours as well. You, in contrast, can impose few expectations on your boss.

As you can see, there are two dimensions to consider: a) the importance or rank of someone who has expectations of you, and b) the range of behavior such expectations may cover. Your spouse or lover may well be able to impose expectations over a broad range of your life, while a boss can reasonably expect you to toe the line only during working hours. Most often, several people have expectations of you. Exactly who they are and how much power they have over you depend on many specifics of your situation.

The main advantage of knowing all this is to help you determine how to react to conflicting expectations or demands. For example, let's suppose you are working at the crucial point of an intricate task you don't want to interrupt. Someone comes in to talk, or to ask that you stop what you're doing and start working on a different project. The best answer is most likely a solid "No." But the answer you actually give depends very much on whether or not that person has a reasonable expectation you will accede to his or her demand.

When two or three people are expressing different expectations at the same time, an uncomfortable conflict results. It may be one of two kinds: a conflict between others over us, or a conflict between ourselves and someone else. You'll handle both of these conflicts more effectively and more comfortably if you know who holds top rank and where you fit in the ranking.

Unfortunately, most of us rank ourselves too low. As a result, you often feel you must give in to other people's demands. You neglect your own preferences, wishes, agendas, and goals in favor of what other people want. Even when justified, this approach makes you less effective because it stops you from working toward your goals. And by definition, you measure effectiveness by your success in reaching your goals.

Keep out of this trap by making sure you know who has legitimate claims on your attention, who can impose expectations on you and who cannot. Use Experience 21 to help you. When someone asks for your help, gives you an order, or urges you to change your agenda to accommodate some new demand, consider all this information before you accept or reject what he or she says. When an inevitable conflict between you and someone else arises, you have a responsibility to yourself to make sure you resolve it with at least one eye to the personal and career goals you want to achieve. Whether you say "Yes" or "No" to what the other person wants, you'll be taking control by making your own decisions about the goals you will pursue and the tasks you will complete.

Experience 21

Self-Evaluation: Interruption Priority and
Communication Priority Lists

Instructions: The object here is to classify all the people who have legitimate claims on your attention into compact lists of people who will: a) always allow, b) sometimes allow, or c) never allow to interrupt you. You can expand the lists to include "types" or "categories" of people whose names you cannot possibly list: salespeople, job applicants, service technicians, and so forth. Even if you have no strong-minded person to enforce your lists for you, the process of compiling them is valuable and can often provide you with the encouragement to do the enforcing yourself.

1) In your personal notebook, list all the people or categories of people you are willing to see whenever they drop by your location, no matter what work or effort you are con- centrating on at the time. Include those who may call on the telephone or send a message.

2) On the next page of your notebook, list all the people or categories of people you are: a) willing to see should they drop by during times you are not busy or concentrating, and b) willing to consider seeing anytime. Include the peo- ple who may call on the telephone or send a message.

3) On the third page, list all the people or categories of peo- ple you are never willing to see. Include those who may call on the telephone or send a message.

4) Update these lists as people and priorities change, and at least once a year. Make copies of your most current lists and pass them to your "enforcer," if you have one.

HOW TO SAY "NO" FIVE EASY WAYS

Saying "No" judiciously is one of the unsung skills of high- powered effectiveness. Naturally, you'll want to say "Yes" many times, not only to be cooperative but to ensure that others will say "Yes" to you when it's important.

Nevertheless, there are many times when a judiciously phrased "No" can save you from minutes, hours, even days of unwanted, unneeded, and unimportant effort. It's the perfect defense against people who want to buy, beg, or borrow your time and effort against your will. But for reasons of politeness, guilt, and much more, many people are reluctant to assert their right to say "No," even when they should. So here are five simple techniques to help you:

a) Just say "No." Actually, saying it is easy: Just open your lips and speak the word. But you probably feel you will lose a lot of friends and acquaintances if you say it too often. And "too often" may actually translate into "once." Nevertheless, saying "No" and meaning it is an extremely useful skill. So practice saying "I'm sorry, but no" to yourself in the mirror. Look yourself right in the eye and say it. Repeat the line two dozen times. After several such sessions, you'll become more used to the sound, and you'll find it easier to turn down someone else when appropriate.

b) Say "No" with a reason. This is easier for most people to accept from you than a refusal that stands alone. For example, you're asked to speak at a neighborhood meeting or to work for some volunteer cause. Say, "No, I'm busy then." Three out of four times, the other person will not press for details. And if you make sure you are busy then, preferably doing something you truly value, you needn't feel guilty about it.

c) Say "No" with a stronger reason. This is the effective response when you are pressed for details. You probably don't have a detailed plan to cite, because then you wouldn't have such a hard time saying "No." But cite one anyway. Say, "No, I have an appointment with my lawyer." This sounds so official that most people will stop right there. Practice making up your own excuses, at least until you have a filled-in schedule that gives you an honest reason to refuse. Note that if you fill your schedule with important activities, you won't have to make up stories or feel bad about saying "No" to less important ones.

d) Say "No" for their own good. Once in a while, you must cloak your refusal in a principle to avoid a chore you don't want. Say, "No, I couldn't give you the quality of results you would want." With this excuse, you're not rejecting the other person's values or commitments. You are merely stating your inadequacy to serve them properly. Despite any objections, you can usually prevail if you are stubborn about this reason. You'll not only avoid the unwanted chore, you'll earn the enviable reputation of one who likes to do a job right or not at all!

e) Say "No" for your own good reasons. This is the final tactic, a "tough guy" attitude with which no one can argue unless you let them. Say, "No, that's not on my list of priorities." You may lose a friend (or gain one), but you will never be thought of as wishy-washy. This statement takes getting used to, particularly when you're the one making it. But it is a stopper, a strong exit line that can save you from most unwanted chores, and even from being asked again at a later date.

All of these variations on "No" require a degree of willpower. You may find it effective to begin with the first variation and say nothing more. Refuse to back it up with explanations, qualifications, ramifications, ifs, ands, or buts. If you do, you'll be back in the same one-way argument you were in before you first tried to say "No."

If the first excuse doesn't end the pressure to say "Yes," move to the second one. Escalate your response to as high a level as necessary to shut off the other person's persistence. If all five won't work, you can still refuse to say the word "Yes." Unless you agree to interrupt your schedule, disregard your priorities, ignore your responsibilities, and do something you don't want to do, no one can actually force you.

CHAPTER 7

MARRIED (OR UNMARRIED) WITH CHILDREN

For most people, raising children is the single most important aspect, or one of the most important aspects, of their lives. If you have children already, you know the special joys they can bring—and the special challenges. This book isn't a parenting primer, but the following section will cover the main aspects of organizing your life for child rearing.

Organizing to raise children is as daunting, as all-encompassing, and as long-range a responsibility as you are likely to encounter in your lifetime. If, as real estate agents like to say, your house is your largest purchase, then surely raising your children is your largest endeavor. But like all great tasks, raising children is made up of hundreds of thousands, perhaps even millions, of tiny chores—each of which virtually any adult can handle. The trick, then, is to set things up so you're in the best possible position and shape to handle each of these chores as it presents itself, and so the unexpected doesn't throw you for a loop.

Since we're not discussing the all-important interpersonal and emotional aspects of child rearing, organizing to raise children entails only five overlapping considerations: time, equipment, travel, other caregivers, and finances. In general, child rearing starts out with babies making very high *quantity* demands for time and equipment. As your children mature, they can get along with less equipment and less—although they usually need a higher *quality*—of your time and attention. Having a fresh diaper available is no longer enough; you need to be ready with answers, advice, direction, and emotional support.

Finances is the one area where children's demands generally increase as they grow older, at least until they leave the nest and begin to support themselves.

As the years go by, encourage your children to help you maintain your organizational scheme and to develop their own. For example, praise and reward your little ones for putting things back where they belong, for planning ahead, and for making more effective Basic Choices. Not all children learn to organize equally well, or equally fast, but the more your children learn to do for themselves, the less you must do for them, and the greater their sense of accomplishment and self-reliance.

ORGANIZING YOUR CHILD-REARING TIME

With young children in the home, time becomes a particularly precious commodity. Most parents continually gain extra time by trading off other aspects of their lifestyles. They may serve packaged baby foods and use a diaper service or disposable diapers. They may buy themselves extra time for work and play by hiring baby-sitters or placing their youngsters in day care.

As you decide whether or not to make these trade-offs, be very aware of your goals and priorities, and how directly you are working toward them. For example, suppose you spend half an hour a week vacuuming your rugs while your child watches TV. As soon as you've finished vacuuming, you drop your child at day care. When you rethink your priorities, though, you may decide to spend some or all of those thirty minutes playing with your child, and either live with dustier rugs or do your vacuuming while your child is out of the house.

Most of the principles, techniques, and practices we've discussed elsewhere in this book apply perfectly well to child rearing, so we've already covered a great deal of ground. However, it's important to emphasize children as a top priority in a parent's life. Spend plenty of time on pursuits like talking to your children, listening when they talk, and trying to understand what they want and need. Just being accessible and available for them is critically important. The process of communicating and sharing with your child—regardless of how much is accomplished in any one session—is a great use of your time. It's also desirable to adjust your own goals and priorities to some degree to accommodate and reflect your children's unique personalities. If they enjoy stamp collecting, spend time with them on this hobby. If they prefer baseball, then make sports a higher priority.

Here's a particularly important point: Most parents find it useful or necessary to *lower their standards* for neatness, orderliness, and on-time scheduling. Children generally require so much time and effort you will simply be unable to perform in these areas as well as you did before you began raising children. Instead, leave more time in your life for relaxation, enjoyment, and recreation away from your routine life and work.

ORGANIZING YOUR CHILD-REARING EQUIPMENT

Friends of mine adopted their two children, and in the process they helped me realize how equipment-oriented the job of parenting has become. One day, my friends left town to claim their new baby boy, and the next day they returned to a house that was totally unequipped for child rearing. Over the next few years, as they grew into their new responsibilities and later adopted a baby girl, their formerly neat and classically decorated home literally blossomed with cribs, playpens, carriages, strollers, diapering gear, toys, high chairs, special bottles, special plates and utensils, special foods, car seats, and so much more.

They not only acquired a great deal of equipment, they rearranged what they already had. They shifted delicate china figurines from coffee tables to an out-of-reach mantle. They regrouped much of their furniture—indoors and out—to make open areas for playpens and sandboxes. They installed "child-safe" latches on cupboards and moved poisons to the top shelves of closets. They began feeding their dog in a closed room, so the children couldn't compete for the pet's daily rations. In short, the house quickly became "child-proof."

Organizing all this equipment makes sense for several reasons. First, you'll find it more cost-effective to get the right equipment and make the best use of it than to buy and use it haphazardly. Second, children are very disorganized, and unless you impose an organizational scheme, your home will quickly become a playhouse unfit and unsuited for adults, and a frustrating place to live. Third, children need so much time and attention that if you can't quickly and easily put your hands on the piece of equipment you need right away, you'll waste hours every day searching for dozens of demanded things—and missing many precious opportunities to have fun with and nurture your children.

But your efforts to organize your children's equipment need not—and should not—interfere with the free flow of love, caring, training, and mutual growth that is at the core of good parenting. Good organization should enhance the parent-child relationship, not infringe upon it.

To begin, try to acquire durable, well-made equipment that will grow with your child (as appropriate). For example, buying an inexpensive playpen for your baby will meet your needs for a year or so, but fairly soon it will break or the child will outgrow it and require another. It's far better to start with a good-quality one that meets all applicable safety standards and will serve you well for all the years you'll use it.

It also makes sense to acquire items that will serve several purposes. Fewer items of equipment will be easier to monitor, maintain, and organize. For example, many baby seats today double as car seats, and there are "seating systems" that also become strollers and high chairs. Children love unbreakable pitchers and cups for bath toys, which are also perfect for rinsing the soap off your child. You'll find a single piece of equipment that meets several needs far more efficient than several single-purpose items.

Another rule I personally enjoyed when our children were young was to emphasize one-piece toys. Naturally, our two boys had a few puzzles, decks of cards, games with dozens of pieces, toy sets that included a multiplicity of parts, and so forth. As we suspected, though, these parts tended to spread throughout the house and cars, or were lost entirely. That's why we came to favor one-piece toys like fire engines, dolls, teddy bears, books, and so forth. I've seen many homes where parents ignore this rule, and generally the floors are littered with objects peremptorily discarded by little ones or made useless by the loss of a crucial part.

It's also important to establish areas in which toys and other items can stay, and areas where toys and child-rearing equipment can only visit. At the end of playtime, or at bedtime, sweep through these "adult" areas and remove everything that doesn't belong. This helps keep certain areas comfortable for grown-ups to spend time in.

Another good time-saver is to store things near where you use them. For example, you probably keep your dishes and eating utensils in the kitchen and your clothing near your bed. So take a lesson from this and keep the child's bathing gear where he or she bathes, the toys in or near the primary play area, the stroller or carriage near the outside door, and so forth.

As kids grow up, their equipment needs change continually. As babies, they need diapers, changes of clothing, liquid or ground-up and strained foods, toys, car seats, strollers, cribs, and much more. After five or six years, they begin to need fewer clothing changes and special foods, but more elaborate toys that challenge their intellects as well as their bodies. As they approach their teens, they can travel much lighter. Like adults, most preteen children will eat readily available foods, and they can go virtually anywhere with just the clothes on their back and perhaps a book or a radio for amusement. As they move through their teenage years, the logistical problems of travel become even simpler because after a while they won't risk the embarrassment of being seen with you. When they do travel with you, they can pack and carry their own clothes and other necessities. However, a teenager's equipment needs can grow to include more expensive items like electric guitars, stereos, a personal telephone line, and an automobile.

ORGANIZING YOUR CHILD-REARING TRAVEL

Even under the best conditions, travel is difficult, expensive, uncomfortable, and stressful. Taking children on the road tends to magnify the difficulties of marshaling the necessary child-rearing equipment. And your children's limited ability to bear the stress and discomfort of travel just makes every problem worse. For my friends with a new baby, a trip to my house—which once had been a spontaneous jaunt in a two-seater sports car—suddenly became a major expedition in a family sedan. It required remembering and physically carrying a car seat, one or two changes of clothing, food and bottles, diapers and a diaper bag, tissues and baby-wipes, toys, perhaps pajamas, a blanket or two, and often much more. Invariably, any item they forgot was the one they most desperately needed that day.

However, after a year or so of experience and careful experiments with different strategies and techniques, my wife and I came to feel fairly unfettered by our children. There were very few places we didn't go because "it would be too much trouble."

Fundamentally, babies are relatively easy to handle and pretty portable. They are light and somewhat predictable, and make only a limited number of demands. As your children mature, they steadily develop stronger personalities and more complex needs.

Day Trips

You can make one-day travel much easier with a little planning and preparation. First, keep a fully packed "baby bag" in the car or stationed just inside your front door. The bag should contain the main items you usually require for a trip with your child. This will change with every child, and with every age, but as parents you'll quickly learn what to pack. Be sure to include a favorite toy, perhaps a special one you bring out only for travel. A small amount of food, such as cookies or crackers packed in a sturdy container to better endure the rigors of travel, will help stem sudden attacks of hunger or unhappiness.

You might also want to maintain a cache of extra supplies in your car—diapers, changes of clothing, entertaining books, games or tapes, perhaps even a pillow and a blanket. With these items prepacked, you won't forget to bring them, no matter where you take your child or how suddenly you depart.

One of the most important, but least considered, types of travel with children is the constant carting you do around your hometown. From their first months, you take extra shopping trips to get them things they need. Later, children create reasons for hundreds of additional trips: to day care and later to school, to various doctors for checkups and treatment of illnesses, to get haircuts, to attend birthday parties, to take dance or music classes, to go to camp and scout meetings, to exchange visits with their friends; and so much more.

Like any trips around town, these excursions should be organized. First, group these destinations as much as possible into a single trip rather than three or four separate ones. Try maintaining shopping lists for various stores you frequently visit, then do all that shopping the next time you're out. This will help you accomplish as much as possible on every trip from home, eliminating special trips to pick up one important item.

Also, if you're dropping off and very soon picking up your child at a lesson, visit, or other appointment, try to make use of this spare time rather than going home and coming back. Find stores nearby to do some necessary shopping, or run some local errands. At least bring a book or some five-minute tasks and avoid wasting the time you must wait.

Extended Travel

At some point in your children's lives, you'll have to begin taking their needs and wants into consideration and adjusting your preferred plans and schedules. As a practical matter, vacations, trips out of town, and other extended travel plans will often require more time, allow for fewer visits and activities, and otherwise reflect your children's limitations. For example, before we had children, my wife and I once drove twelve hours to get home from a visit to a friend in North Carolina. We didn't plan to. It just felt right, so we did it. With small children along, such a free-spirited last-minute decision (and the resulting endurance marathon) would have been impossible.

For most young children, an hour or two between rest stops is the practical limit, and three or four hours of travel may be the most they can handle in a single day. When possible, limit each day's travel time to an hour less than your children have shown they can endure. Also, plan events and visits to points of interest they will like, and fit these in between your own events and visits. Occasionally, you may want to split up, with one parent going off with one child, or send the children off to an amusement park, mall, or sporting event for a few hours. When you visit family or friends, your children can go off or stay with grandparents, aunts and uncles, other friends, or hired baby-sitters.

For car trips, we found a successful formula that may work for you, too: Start out immediately after breakfast. After two hours or so (when the children generally become restless), take a half-hour break and do something active and fun. Drive a while farther and break for lunch. Drive some more, then call a halt in the early afternoon. We'd try to finish near a playground, zoo, or other attraction where the children could burn off their pent-up energy. Later, we'd spend the rest of the day just amusing ourselves with toys, decks of cards, games, books, slow walks, and family fun. We didn't get as far as we could have without the kids, but we avoided angry or frustrating situations and we enjoyed ourselves.

When the children are young, you may all be able to sleep in one motel or hotel room. As they mature, though, you may prefer to rent an adjoining room so your children can have their own bedtimes, and so you can have some peace and quiet. It's also more convenient to have more than one bathroom available. Certain hotels cater to families with children, and many offer discounts to families, such as a cheaper second room or free breakfasts in the hotel.

On extended trips, meals can become a real problem. Prepare for this from the beginning by encouraging your children to eat civilly in a variety of restaurants. From the moment they can sit up by themselves, begin praising and rewarding them for sitting quietly in restaurants, for selecting something they want from the menu, for waiting patiently until it is served, and then for eating it neatly and without a fuss. During their first few years, you'll have very little success—I remember a two-week vacation with our first child when we ate every meal in pancake houses—but as the years pass, your children will become better suited to eating in places you appreciate.

Airplane travel is particularly difficult for families. Babies often cry or become cranky. Small children can become bored or rambunctious, and may suffer ear pain on takeoff or landing. To avoid these problems, prepare and plan in advance. Pack a steady supply of toys, games, decks of cards, tapes, or books. Bring something for them to chew, as this helps relieve air-pressure differences in their ears. Experiment with nonstop and stopover flights. Nonstops minimize the number of takeoffs and landings, and get the airplane trip out of the way as quickly as possible. The shorter hops may provide time to rest and relax on the layovers, and the extra variety of activity can help keep the children occupied.

ORGANIZING YOUR CHILDREN'S CAREGIVERS

Whether it's grandparents who take the kids on a Sunday afternoon, neighborhood baby-sitters, part-time housekeepers, full-time nannies, day-care and preschool workers, or teachers at school, caregivers are an important part of any child's life. Also, as your children grow older, you may want to give them valuable experiences and chances to develop independence at day camp and overnight camp. Because these caregivers are substitute parents, they must be capable of keeping your children safe and sound, and must also fall within acceptable limits regarding the ideas, values, and experiences to which they will expose your impressionable young ones.

It's not always possible or desirable for you to stop working so you can raise your own children full-time. But it is possible to better organize and control their environment when you are not around.

First, of course, you must know what you want for your child: the values, the experiences, and the training you want to provide. Although complete agreement on every detail is relatively rare, both parents can and must achieve some practical level of consensus so your child does not become the battleground in a parental tug-of-war.

If you have more than one child, understand that each is different and may require support and guidance in different areas of growing up. One may be irresponsible, another may feel too responsible. One may be antisocial, another may be too dependent on winning approval from others. Some children need special help to grow up happy, healthy, and independent.

Next, discuss your desired values, experiences, and training goals with each caregiver. Do it *before* you hand over responsibility to them.

Often with grandparents, you can't much change what they will say and do. But most children are relatively safe with grandparents. Most children are also fairly safe with baby-sitters and others who spend only a few hours with them—provided you've used considerable precautions in screening and checking references.

The first concern is personal safety. Make sure the caregiver is competent and mature, with good judgment. He or she should know what to do and whom to call in case of injury, accident, or illness. Once you feel comfortable with this, turn your attention to other concerns.

A five-day-a-week caregiver, for example, will inevitably create an emotional environment in which your child will do a lot of growing up. Even a few afternoons a week is enough to have significant influence. Someone who panics easily, or who responds with anger to every surprise or problem, can leave an indelible mark on your child's psyche. Other styles of emotional response or strongly held points of view can also have an influence. At least be aware of the possibilities. In extreme cases, you may want to change caregivers to avoid a potential problem.

Be sure to monitor your child's activities with caregivers, too. Does your child spend the time watching TV or taking walks in the park? It does make a difference. If necessary, develop a schedule and arrange for certain activities so your child is reared—at least to some extent—the way you would like it done.

Most day-care centers, preschools, and schools provide ample opportunities for parents to discuss philosophies, observe ongoing sessions, and monitor daily activities. If you're lucky, you'll feel good about leaving your child at the facility. But if the demand in your neighborhood far exceeds the supply, you may feel great pressure to accept less-than-perfect child care. Even if you have no choice, however, you can often improve the situation. Take the time to get involved in the process. Visit now and again. Meet frequently with the people who will directly care for your child. Show your concern; ask questions. By presenting a nonthreatening, cooperative attitude, you can usually influence the daily flow of values, ideas, and activities more toward what you prefer for your child.

ORGANIZING YOUR CHILD-REARING FINANCES

This book is not heavily concerned with financial matters, but they are important in this context because children tend to be expensive. A century ago, a child was a source of profit: an extra set of hands to work on the family farm, or to be apprenticed to a craftsperson and thus earn wages for the family. Today, a child is much more likely to be an unremitting expense until he or she leaves home. The little ones require food, clothing, health care, and the occasional toy. As they get older, their demands become more costly. If they attend college, you can easily spend many tens of thousands of dollars on this final phase of child rearing. When the economy slows down, young people are often the first to be laid off, which often forces them to return home until they find another job.

Although it's often said "babies bring their own luck," you'll feel a lot luckier about raising your children once you start planning and saving for their future. Many types of long-term bonds or mutual funds require contributions of only a few dollars at a time, yet offer huge returns over a child's growth to maturity. If you can afford to save only $10 a week for your child, and can earn just 5 percent per year on this money, after twenty-one years you can write your child a birthday check in the amount of $19,304.58. Your total cash outlay will have been only $10,920. The extra $8,384.58 results from your early planning and organizing of these financial matters. Here's more proof: If you wait until your child's third birthday before you start this savings program, on that same twenty-first birthday your check will be for (only) $15,168.81. Which check would you rather write?

One of the simplest ways to start organizing this part of your financial situation is to set goals, calculate the contributions required to reach these goals, and make the arrangements as automatic as possible. For example, suppose your goal is to accumulate $100,000 in twenty-one years. We can calculate that at 5 percent interest this requires a $52 contribution every week. You could write a check or make a cash deposit every week. But it's simpler—and less likely to be skipped—if you arrange for your bank or broker to withdraw $52 from your main account every week, or $225 every month. You can change the arrangement any time you wish, of course, but you'll probably want to let it run its course, accumulating money without any further thought on your part. Most mutual funds, banks, and brokerage houses can make such an arrangement for you, virtually guaranteeing you'll meet financial child-rearing goals.

Another aspect of organizing your finances for child rearing is to secure sufficient life insurance. Generally, life insurance is best used to replace the income lost when a wage earner dies prematurely. The insurance creates enough of a nest egg to replace the income the insured no longer provides. You might feel staggered by the capital required to generate as much income as your family will need over the next couple of decades, and the cost of that much insurance. But balance this expense against the image of your children suffering for want of money. Suddenly, the insurance premium may look much more reasonable. I advise you to buy life insurance and hope your family never needs it.

There's a great deal more you can do with regard to finances, but all of it is subject to the same ideas, principles, and practices we've covered elsewhere in this book. Set your goals and priorities, plan the necessary activities, and carry out your plan. The biggest problem is that most people procrastinate on their financial planning, hoping they'll have more leisure time and extra money later on. There are rarely—if ever—positive aspects to procrastinating on this important responsibility. The longer you delay, the more you miss those extra years of accumulating interest and profit that will mean so much when your children come of age and when you retire. It's far more effective to do your financial planning at the earliest possible moment, not wait for a convenient one.

WHEN PARENTS LIVE APART

Our discussion so far has not addressed situations where parents live apart, such as after a separation or divorce, or after the death of one parent. There is also a growing trend for single people to intentionally raise children without a partner. These situations can easily become very complicated. Child rearing is enormously difficult for single parents: There's no letup in responsibilities, and no one to offset your emotional ups and downs, scheduling conflicts, illnesses, or exhaustion. A single parent often feels extra pressure to "do a good job," too, to make up for the obvious deficiencies in the family structure.

Since this book is not intended to cover emotional, legal, or other issues, our main concern is logistical: how to organize the time, equipment, travel, parental surrogates, and finances when you live at a distance from your child; when you require cooperation from your child's other parent, who lives elsewhere; or when there is no other parent to share your burdens.

Let's first assume that your child is with you and the other parent lives apart, or that there is no other parent. Essentially, you're in control. Happily, a good deal of parenting is accomplished in the myriad tiny decisions of "Where do we go now?" and "What do we do in the next minute?" Get yourself organized along the lines we've discussed throughout this book. Establish your goals. Take action to achieve those goals. Concentrate on your top priorities. Marshal your resources for child rearing, and help your child organize him- or herself. If the other parent is in the picture and has a problem or makes demands, you'll be in a strong position to respond in ways that make sense for you and your children.

Most times, these problems involve larger issues that carry great emotional weight, and perhaps considerable practical importance as well. For example, more than one mother and daughter have been hampered in almost every aspect of life by a distant father who refuses to pay adequate alimony or child support. Fathers raising their children have suffered from distant mothers who regularly dump emotional baggage on their children and leave the father to sort things out. There can frequently be disagreements over other subjects: visiting rights, friends and live-in lovers, schools, religious upbringing, extracurricular activities, and so forth.

Few separated parents can resolve these problems easily, usually for some of the same reasons they originally separated: failure to agree on basics. Nevertheless, you can make a lot of progress toward agreement by first understanding exactly what you want from the situation, then by developing a list of potential or desirable tasks that lead you toward these goals, and finally by working toward these objectives one by one, in some cases negotiating and pressuring the distant parent to help you.

For example, if you're disagreeing on where to send your child to school, first decide on the school you prefer, then establish your reasons for this and decide how to communicate the advantages of this school to the other parent. Finally, start working to drive home the importance of these advantages.

Naturally, some of these disagreements are never going to be resolved, because one or both parties don't want them resolved. Unfortunately, one or both parents often see the child as the best weapon with which to get their way. But it's almost always very unhealthy for the child, and for the parents, to use this approach.

Instead, deal directly with the distant parent and understand that your child—even after the age of twenty-one—may not be equipped emotionally to enter into your relationship as a full-fledged member. At all times, remember who is the parent and who is the child. Encourage all parties—including yourself—to play their appropriate roles.

Weekending

Weekends can be a difficult time for children of separated or single parents. You want to get away, or you want your child to get away, as smoothly and happily as possible.

Make it simpler by learning from past experiences. Keep a list of necessary items—from diapers and pacifiers (for babies) to toiletries and favorite CDs (for older children). Keep adding to the list as you learn from sad experiences, and then pack your child's suitcase with the list in front of you. As your child gets older, encourage him or her to take more and more responsibility for packing, making travel arrangements, and remaining in control of emotions and actions while away from home.

Living in Two Houses

Separated families create immense organizational problems. If your child simply visits his or her other parent for a short time, the problem boils down to "taking a vacation" without you. But if his or her time is substantially split between the two parents, the organizational problems become much more significant.

Emotions aside, having your child move out for a while will probably simplify your life. But he or she may need a certain amount of continuity. Packing clothes and equipment can become a major undertaking, almost to the extent of "moving house" once or twice a year. You may also want to make time to visit your child in the "other home," and help him or her get acclimated to the differences. Also consider whether you must arrange for school and medical records to be forwarded, for example, and whether you want to supply your child with preaddressed postcards or envelopes so he or she can more easily write to you.

If your child is coming to you, consider where he or she will sleep. What about clothing? School or camp? Friends? Activities? The presence of your child may alter your lifestyle with regard to meals, bedtimes, daytime and evening activities, travel, finances, and everything else. So be ready to remain flexible, accept necessary adjustments, and make the best of the situation.

Make the whole experience as easy as possible by planning ahead, by getting an early start on what must be done, and by leaving time in your plan for last-minute changes and unanticipated requirements.

Developing Other Resources

One of the best ways to improve your situation as a single parent is to develop a strong support structure to take some of the unrelenting burden off your shoulders. This might include a single-parent support group, a school-based parenting group, the families of your child's friends, or your own friends. See Chapter 6 for ideas on how to build and maintain strong relationships with people who can help you in this way.

Many people who have children of their own, or who don't have children, or whose children are grown, are happy to help single parents by taking the child(ren) for an afternoon, an overnight stay, or a weekend. They not only give you a needed respite, they provide other role models and experiences for your child(ren).

CHAPTER 8

A CONCISE PROGRAM FOR THE BUSY BUSINESS EXECUTIVE

This is a concise program to help the overworked executive do more in less time and focus very accurately on his or her most important objectives. It's a step-by-step guide to take you from your present work habits and time-use patterns to a more useful, more streamlined, more effective system. But the value you obtain from this program depends directly on how much specific detail you use in your responses to the questions and how long you stay with any changes to which the program leads you.

Go through the program slowly but steadily at first, carefully completing each step before going on to the next. Make a note on your calendar to go through the program again in a month. You'll go faster the second time, since you will already have prepared your lists and become familiar with the concepts. You'll also see what improvements the program has brought you, and have a chance to correct any errors or old habits creeping back into your days.

MEASURE YOUR PRESENT RESULTS

Step 1: List Responsibilities

Use Experience 22 to briefly review your job description, your career history, and your personal goals to determine what areas deserve your best efforts. For example, a sales manager might have the following:

a) Job responsibilities: to supervise twenty-three sales people, approve expense-account expenditures, and help set sales quotas
b) Career goals: to keep abreast of current developments in the industry, prepare for promotion, and develop relationships with key managers in the sales organization
c) personal goals: to stay in good physical condition, develop an interesting carry-over hobby for retirement, and read one new novel a month

Experience 22

Your Responsibilities

1)   In your personal notebook, list your present job-related, career-related, and personal responsibilities.
2)   For each responsibility, note the number of hours each week you feel it requires.
3)   For each responsibility, note what time of day or day of the week you might prefer (or find it most efficient) to work toward this responsibility.
4)   For each responsibility, note the amount of time you actually spend on it (from notes you keep for this purpose

and/or from Time Log entries, as explained in Appendix A).

Step 2: Determine Work Habits and Time-Use Patterns

The most accurate way to spot your work habits and time-use patterns is through a Time Log. (Details of Time Log techniques are discussed in Appendix A. Estimating procedures are given at the end of this chapter.) For now, go ahead with the concise program using estimates. Next time, use the more accurate figures from your Time Logs.

HOW TO ESTABLISH YOUR PRIORITIES

Step 3: Indicate Your Preferences

When you are satisfied you know your work habits and time-use patterns, go through the list you created in Experience 22 and indicate (by initials or other simple codes) whether you would prefer to spend more, less, or just about the same time working toward each responsibility.

As you indicate your preferences, take into account what each responsibility is worth to you when achieved, that is, the payoffs or benefits you will receive when you fulfill the responsibility. Consider immediate payoffs, of course, as well as any long-term skills, contacts, or other benefits this effort may bring in the future.

Step 4: Calculate Time Needs

Next to each responsibility you listed in Experience 22 write down its *minimum* requirement per day or week—the figure below which you cannot accomplish anything useful. Some items, like physical exercise, may have a minimum of thirty minutes three times a week. Others, like reading or listening to music for pleasure, may bring benefits in even the smallest amounts. Also, write down an *optimum* figure—the amount of time that offers the best balance of time, effort, and results.

For example, imagine you are responsible for overseeing your company's credit union. The minimum effort here might be five hours per month. Any less, and you have no chance to keep on top of the credit union's outstanding loans and investments. The optimum effort might be ten hours per month: enough to handle routine oversight, with a small cushion of time for emergencies or some of the more desirable and important opportunities.

Thinking about minimum and optimum time requirements will help you allocate your time and effort more meaningfully, and more effectively, among your full range of responsibilities. They define a range of *time needs* that help you avoid putting too much or too little attention toward any single responsibility.

HOW TO BEGIN PLANNING YOUR DAYS AND WEEKS

Step 5: Parcel Out Your Energy

When you have studied your responsibilities, including each one's realistic *time needs,* and your preferences, you can begin deciding which objectives to work toward first. To begin with, allocate your time among your most important responsibilities, then block out time for items of lesser priority.

A good way to accomplish more of your most important or most satisfying objectives is to block them in on your calendar before any others. Use their *optimum time needs* as guidelines.

Get a large wall or desk calendar with ample write-in room for each day. Block out the exact hours and dates for working toward each responsibility. For example, say a portion of your list of responsibilities has these new allocations:

1.	Weekly performance report	8 hours
2.	Monthly performance report	2 hours
3.	Development of product X	20 hours
4.	Coordination of departments	15 hours
5.	Test marketing of product Y	8 hours

You might block out time for them as follows:

Date	Responsibility	Hours
8/1	1. Weekly report	9–11
	2. Monthly report	1–3
8/2	3. Development of X	9–11
	4. Coordination	1–3
8/3	5. Marketing of Y	9–11
	5. Marketing of Y	1–3
8/8	1. Weekly report	9–11
	3. Development of X	1–4
8/9	5. Marketing of Y	9–11
	4. Coordination	1–4

The pattern here is a good one. It includes two- and 3-hour blocks of time reserved for specific important purposes. It leaves holes in the schedule for routines and daily activities, unexpected developments, and last-minute changes. Most important, it puts major responsibilities on the calendar first, before routines and "urgent" trivia can crowd them off.

If you can, stay scheduled at least two months, and for some tasks as much as a year, into the future.

Treat this allocation as a first approximation only, making adjustments from time to time as your priorities and your responsibilities evolve. Setting your own allocations this way gives you more control over your results and helps you maximize the results you obtain. Over the long run, you'll achieve more of what you want, be more effective, productive, and satisfied.

Step 6: Follow Your Schedule

This advance scheduling gives you a solid basis on which to work toward fulfilling your major responsibilities early enough to meet your deadlines. If you follow the schedule, you won't have to disrupt the smooth flow of work to make a last-minute rush for completion.

But none of this will do much good if you allow yourself to fall back on your present work habits and time-use patterns. It's not enough just to mark your calendar—you must also strive to follow the schedules you mark. If you fall behind or deviate too much from this idealized schedule, you're ignoring at least some of your primary responsibilities. Try to isolate the causes; try even harder to get back on schedule. Although you may have trouble breaking old work habits and time-use patterns, you'll enjoy tremendous benefits when you finally begin to put more of your effort toward your most important goals.

Step 7: Regularly Rate Your Performance

Check your results and achievements at the end of each month. See if you are working when and how you planned. Give yourself a rating from 1 to 10 for:

a) Fulfillment of responsibilities   _____
b) Completion of work on time   _____
c) Useful allocation of effort   _____
d) Satisfaction with new system   _____
e) This month's accomplishments   _____

If you are satisfied with your results, stick with the program and see how much more you can achieve by directing more and more of your efforts toward the goals you really want. If you are not satisfied, don't give up. Redouble your efforts to make an effective schedule and to stick to it.

TEN GREAT EFFECTIVENESS BUILDERS YOU CAN USE IMMEDIATELY

1) The Office Meeting

Coordination and cooperation are big problems in most organizations. If one person doesn't get word of a decision or a vital bit of information, weeks of work by many people can go down the drain. Also, isolation and lack of communication can reduce morale, weaken loyalties, and seriously interrupt your group's effectiveness.

Used judiciously, the office meeting can be the antidote to all of this. It is simply a regularly scheduled get-together in your office, or somewhere close by, during which everyone has a chance to listen and talk about current work issues. In-group and out-group feelings can be short-circuited by inviting everyone to the office meeting.

The agenda for the meeting should be well planned to include:

a) Current items of interest
b) Brief reports from people on how their work is going
c) Discussions of problems coordinating people
d) Brief discussions of projects and problems to come

The meeting should be as concise and well ordered as possible, should start promptly on schedule, and should be conducted with a brisk air of busy people eager to get something important accomplished and get on to something else equally or more important.

Two variations on this meeting include the daily meeting with your secretary and the weekly or biweekly meeting with your most important subordinates. Again, these ought to be regular, brisk sessions at which the major business is to communicate fully and thereby coordinate the upcoming work.

2) A Wall or Desk Calendar

Already mentioned in this concise program, a wall or desk calendar is a valuable organizing tool for any executive with several irons simultaneously in the fire.

Place your wall or desk calendar where you can see it easily, and write on it large enough so you can read it from your usual position. (Computer software now permits you to automate all these scheduling techniques. If you use your computer frequently, as I do, you may agree with me that software provides a better alternative to the traditional paper-and-pencil methods.)

Fill in your calendar yourself, or give your secretary or assistant the task of filling it in for you. Keep noting items on your calendar as far into the future as you can. Use pencil for tentative dates;

bold marker for important objectives you want to meet. You can also use colors to designate certain standard kinds of work. For example: red for budget planning, blue for reporting efforts, green for appointment, and orange for reading or thinking time.

Check your calendar frequently to see what's coming up later this week and next. Use these cues to get ready mentally, to assemble needed materials and information, and to advise anyone you'll be working with of the upcoming scheduled effort. Also check your calendar before adding new commitments. This way, you won't overload a certain week and leave other days with virtually nothing important on tap.

3) The Quiet Hours

A great device for getting more work done in a given period of time. The key to success with a Quiet Hour is cooperation: Everyone within earshot obeys the Quiet Hour rules. Most Quiet Hours are established from 8 to 9 or 9 to 10 A.M., or from 3 to 4 or 4 to 5 P.M. The specific hour you choose matters very little so long as everyone cooperates to make it work.

The basic rules of the Quiet Hour are:

a) No unnecessary talking, walking, or moving around
b) No loud noise of any kind
c) No incoming or outgoing calls or visits
d) Everyone concentrating on his or her most important activities for the full Quiet Hour

It's best when everyone participates in the Quiet Hour. However, a minimum number of receptionists may be needed to deal with visitors and take telephone messages.

There is a problem with the Quiet Hour, however. Many people do not like to be put off when they call you or come in. Whether bringing nothing to say or news of a big emergency, every individual believes his or her message is important and deserves immediate consideration. You can overcome this problem, of course, but it requires a two-pronged effort of education and good manners.

Print up notices for all the people who commonly call during your Quiet Hour. It can say something like:

We are instituting a Quiet Hour from 9 to 10 A.M. every day. During this hour, we will not accept visitors or telephone calls. Our purpose is to concentrate our efforts and get more work accomplished. Since our Quiet Hour will result in better and faster service to you and everyone who does business with us, we hope you will understand our procedure and our need for it. Thank you.

In addition, you can make special arrangements for callers to get through when they have legitimate needs to talk to you immediately. One way is through a special "hotline" that is answered even during Quiet Hours. Or you can give your special callers a "code" that signals your receptionist or your voice mail system to put them through. Too many exceptions, however, will circumvent the whole purpose of the Quiet Hour.

4) Dictation Techniques

Dictating is three to eight times faster than longhand writing, depending on the relative speeds of your wrist and your thoughts. If you are already dictating, think about doing more of it. If you haven't yet switched over, consider it now.

Dictation is useful for:

- Writing reports
- Handling correspondence and memos
- Taking notes on phone conversations
- Taking notes on meetings
- Capturing random thoughts and "bright ideas"
- Giving instructions to distant staff
- Sending your voice on tape to lend a personal touch to long-distance communications
- Improving speeches by verbalizing your ideas instead of drafting them
- Working while driving or otherwise traveling

The basics of successful dictation include good equipment, good technique, and practice. There are many dictating machines on the market, with many features and varying degrees of portability.

Investigate several and get a machine that does what you want and need.

Dictate from an outline, not off the top of your heard. Prepare a list of points you want to cover, and then dictate your elaborations on each one in turn. Also, prepare in advance by doing your research, reading, and most especially your thinking before you turn on the machine. Then you'll have the ideas all ready and can simply voice them. At first, use dictation just for an initial draft. You needn't make it perfect, because you'll correct a typed transcript and polish your prose in print. After a while, though, you won't need to review short items like letters, memos, and notes; your initial dictation will be good enough. If you have the knack, you may gain enough skill to dictate longer manuscripts without seeing or correcting a draft version.

Take your machine with you when you can. The more you use it, the more effective you will be. Get in the habit of carrying a pocket-size recorder in your car, on walks, to the tennis court, even to bed—anywhere and everywhere your mind is active. Record any thoughts you think worth saving. Have them typed up for your later review, modification, or disposal. (If you don't have a secretary, hire a transcription service.)

5) Preprinted Communicators

You can speed your communication efforts if you prepare pre-printed versions of your answers to the most common inquiries. You can also print up: routing slips, inquiry letters, form statements of procedure, descriptive materials, lists of satisfied customers, address labels, and so forth—anything you write or say more than once can probably be duplicated effectively. See Chapter 4 for more details on this technique.

6) Work Flowcharts

Visual representation of the work in your office can be a great help. It lets you smooth that flow, coordinate elements better, and plan your work so you are ready for each step when it's due. See the "Sample Flowchart (with Deadlines) for Film Project," which shows the visual representation of a film project from initial con-

for a tendency to overestimate, or "enhance," these figures. Remember, no one is looking over your shoulder at this accounting. Try to make the figures as representative of your true actions as you can.

These estimates of your time spent on various activities can be used in various Experiences in this book. But start keeping a Time Log at your earliest opportunity, as you will find those figures far more accurate than any estimates you can make.

CHAPTER 11

A BASIC ACHIEVEMENT PROGRAM FOR EVERYONE WHO HAS A MISSION OR A DREAM

If you've read through this book from the beginning, you now have some strong ideas on how to control your results by working first and foremost on your most important and satisfying opportunities. If you haven't read the whole book, a great deal of useful material awaits you. This chapter is intended to give you a "jump start" toward effectiveness by synthesizing and incorporating many of the book's ideas and techniques into a specific procedure you can use to accomplish any mission or dream you have in mind. Appendix C gives you more details to help you carry out this procedure.

SUMMARY OUTLINE OF PROGRAM

1. Define your mission or your dream.

   a. Establish clear descriptions of what you want
   b. Develop one or more goals in support of what you want
   c. Break down each goal into activities, with deadlines
   d. Develop firm yardsticks for evaluating success
   e. Identify the specific rewards you will obtain

2. Identify the Major Steps needed to achieve your goal.

   a. Consider each clear advance a Major Step toward your goal
   b. Identify the Major Steps you must achieve and put them in sensible order
   c. Identify the reward you'll gain from each accomplishment

3. Organize each Major Step.

   a. Set a deadline for completion
   b. Identify the Minor Steps in each Major Step
   c. Put the Minor Steps in sensible order
   d. Identify or establish a reward for each Minor Step

4. Organize each Minor Step.

   a. Break each one into one-day (or one-hour) tasks
   b. Put the tasks in sensible order
   c. Identify or establish a reward for completing each task

5. Schedule each one-hour task.

   a. Definitely do at least one every day
   b. Accept and enjoy the rewards you earn

6. Cross off the Steps you have completed.

   a. Accept and enjoy this further reward

7. Share your method with others, to:
   a. Gain extra stimulation
   b. Win extra admiration
   c. Motivate you to work more toward your goal

8. Thoroughly enjoy each goal when you achieve it.

As long as you follow the principles and ideas in this book, and then apply them and the accompanying techniques to your special situations, you WILL achieve your dream. I guarantee it! Here's what you must do:

KNOW YOUR MISSION OR DREAM, AND YOUR GOALS

Your personal mission or dream, is a large-scale accomplishment that may constitute all—or a significant part—of your life's work. Once you have a mission or a dream, you can usually discover one or more significant goals within it that will help you toward achieving your ultimate aim. Defining these goals, then actively working toward them, is the key to achieving your mission. If you set impossible goals, you doom yourself to failure, but a goal you can reach gives you a solid start toward eventual success.

However, just having one or more goals you can reach does not automatically guarantee success. A great many motivational and self-image considerations also strongly affect what you achieve— when, how, and why. The first part of this chapter seeks to explore your relation to your mission and your goals, without attempting to dictate your answers. There are no "right" or "wrong" responses, just honest ones. Here are your first steps toward achieving your mission and your goals.

1) Define Your Mission or Your Dream Clearly

Do this in enough detail that others can recognize what you want. If you cannot do this, yours is probably an impossible dream.

For example, a certain eager businessman—we'll call him John— got the idea for a new and extremely useful household appliance.

Instead of selling separate electric can openers, blenders, food processors, mixers, and coffee grinders—each with its separate small motor—John would sell all the appliances together as attachments to one very powerful and efficient motor.

John began development and made rapid progress. But then he wondered, "Why settle for five attachments? Six would be even better." So development continued, and again the product took shape. But again John wanted to make changes.

The process went on for months until his investors began to suspect John's dream would always outstrip product development. John had no chance to achieve his goal because he let it expand and change faster than he made progress.

You protect yourself against the dangers of such impossible dreams by defining your dream very clearly. Although you can always change your mind, if this happens too often you may recognize that your dream is retreating out of reach. You can still choose between grabbing the satisfying, attainable goal you've already defined or continuing to pursue an impossible dream. At least you have given yourself the choice.

2) Set Up a Deadline for Achieving Your Dream

Give yourself enough time, but keep the deadline near enough so you feel some pressure to start toward it now. You may want to schedule in reverse from your final target date, and thus establish a plan that can get you moving today toward accomplishing your mission or your dream.

3) Set Specific Criteria

In this way, you will recognize when you achieve your dream. The more concrete, specific, and objective you make these criteria, the more easily you can check your progress toward your dream.

For example, a newly married couple had the dream of "being wealthy." Though they set their hearts on a yearly income that they thought would make them happy, they recognized that inflation would make this income seem steadily smaller every few years. So they established other, more timeless criteria to measure their wealth: a) feeling comfortable hiring domestic help, b) feeling comfortable dining in the most expensive restaurants in town, c) not feeling concerned about the money needed for their everyday expenses.

Seven years later, both had become successful in their fields. They earned the income they had dreamed of. But strictly on the basis of their dollar income, they did not feel as wealthy as they had wanted to be. However, their other criteria convinced them. Because they could meet those well-defined criteria, they knew they had reached their goal!

In a similar case, an athletic young man wanted to become a long-distance bicycle racer. He set up some specific criteria for the distances he wanted to go, the level of competition he wanted to meet, and approximate times he wanted to beat. Years later, when he could meet his own standards, he knew he had done what he wanted.

Calculate the Rewards Your Dream Achievement Will Bring You

Missions or dreams are usually not easy to accomplish. You need extra motivation and perseverance. To get more of both, calculate the good things and feelings that will flow to you once you accomplish what you want.

For example, if your dream is great wealth, think about the relationships and opportunities your wealth will bring you. If fame, think about all the glory and glamour of great popularity. You probably do this already; it's the natural way most people cherish their dreams. But for this exercise, do this type of thinking more practically.

And focus on possible negative results or disappointments, too. For example, a great swimming star spent years training for his ultimate competitive event. Although in the water he achieved all he wanted and a great deal more, only two days after his triumph he began feeling depressed, bored, and empty. He got less satisfaction from his achievement than he expected, and it brought him responsibilities and burdens he didn't enjoy. Perhaps if he had thoroughly explored his own expectations, and the objective pros and cons of his goal, he might have been better prepared for his ultimate "success."

So don't define just your goal in great detail. Define—in just as much detail—the rewards and possible problems that will flow from achieving it. Write them down, as you're instructed to do in Experience 25, so you can refer to the list later on.

Experience 25

Define Your Dream

Instructions: In your personal notebook, record your mission or your dream that you plan to accomplish.

1) Specify a deadline by which you feel you can achieve your mission or dream.
3) Specify objective criteria so you or anyone else can recognize when you have accomplished your mission or dream.
3) List all the rewards and benefits you expect to receive (and enjoy) from accomplishing your mission or dream. List any negative results that may flow from achieving your dream.
4) Consider how you will feel after achieving your dream. How will you feel if you find that the negative results outweigh the positive ones?

SPECIFY THE MAJOR STEPS

You have explored your attitudes, expectations, and feelings about your dream in Experience 25. Now you can turn to a more active phase of the achievement program. Use Experience 26 to list all the major accomplishments that together add up to the achievement of your dream.

For example, one famous actress felt strongly that she wanted a chance to direct feature films. She listed the major accomplishments necessary to achieving this dream as follows:

a) Gain credibility as a director by accumulating academic credentials and practical training
b) Make two or three short films to practice techniques and prove my talent

    c) Find a good story or script
    d) Use my contacts and knowledge of the industry to get a
       major producer to back me
    e) Make the film

She followed her plan, and after eight years achieved her goal.

If you have little or no experience in planning, you may feel stymied at this point in the program. You needn't be. Breaking down large goals into smaller ones is a very simple and direct process. Here's one way to dissect your dream into Major Steps:

    a) Specify the people, equipment, information, skills, facili-
       ties, space and/or locations that are necessary to achieve
       your dream.
    b) Let the process of acquiring each of these count as a Ma-
       jor Step.
    c) Let the process of putting all the elements together to
       achieve the goal count as an additional Major Step.

The differences between the Major Steps and the Minor Steps (which you'll specify later) are subtle but definite. A Major Step is an *accomplishment* that brings certain desired results. In a way, it is a goal in itself. For example, it would be a Major Step on the road to the Presidency to become Governor of your state, because this brings you political power and experience. It would not be a Major Step to work out your positions on various presidential issues, because this brings you no real results. Results from several Major Steps combine to bring you to the realization of your dream.

A Minor Step is an *action* you take toward achieving a Major Step, and counts regardless of whether or not it brings you the results you expected. For example, a Minor Step on the road to the Presidency would be writing a position paper describing your views on the issues, or undertaking an expensive publicity campaign. Such an action counts as a Minor Step whether or not it produces any results. For this reason, there is no limit to the number of Minor Steps that could combine to make up just one Major Step.

In your plan, describe each Major Step as fully as you described your original dream or mission, with a detailed description and several objective criteria so you'll know when you have achieved it. Once you have a list of Major Steps, put them in sensible order. The most common sequence is chronological, from the first to the last. You'll find that some of the Steps clearly fit before or after certain others. For example, the screen actress had to establish her credibility before she could expect to get backing as a director. But you can try to accomplish certain Steps in almost any order. That's why she could reasonably expect to find a good story or screenplay at any time.

To handle this slightly confusing situation, place your Major Steps on one of two lists. The first list should contain all the Steps that are strictly chronological. The second should contain all the Steps you can reasonably do at any point in the process. You may want to put this second list of Major Steps in some other sequence, such as from the simplest to most difficult, or from the least expensive to the most expensive.

Now refer to Experience 26 and to your own imagination. Try to tie each of your Major Steps to a satisfying reward you will get when you complete it. This motivational trick really works. And while it may seem a little silly, tedious, or contrived, you will never know its value until you put it into action. Believe me, it will work.

Experience 26

The Major Accomplishments of Your Dream Goal

Instructions: In your personal notebook, identify your Dream Goal and organize the Major Steps required to accomplish it.

1) List the Major Steps required to accomplish your Dream Goal.
2) Put the Major Steps in chronological order. Make two separate lists: one for Steps you must do in order, and a second for Steps you can try to do anytime.
3) Number the Steps in the two lists, and for each number, specify a reward you will receive upon finishing that Step.

PLAN EACH MAJOR STEP

Each of the Major Steps in your dream goal deserves its own miniplan. For each of your Major Steps, establish a directed series of efforts to accomplish it. Use Experience 27 to help you create:

a) A deadline for completing the Major Step
b) A series of Minor Steps required to achieve it
c) A sensible order for the Minor Steps
d) A satisfying reward you will receive when you accomplish each Minor Step

---

Experience 27

Organizing Each Major Step

Instructions: In your personal notebook, list a Major Step and the dream goal toward which it will lead you. Then organize the Major Step. Use a separate page for each Major Step.

1) Set a deadline for the achievement of the Major Step.
2) List the Minor Steps you must take to achieve the Major Step you're planning.
3) Put the Minor Steps above into sensible order. Make two lists: one for Steps you must do in order, and a second one for Steps you can try to do anytime.
4) Number the Minor Steps you've listed, and for each number, specify a reward you will receive (or give yourself) from accomplishing each.

PLAN EACH MINOR STEP

You can find the Minor Steps of your program by looking for actions you must take to achieve each Major Step. For example, if a Major Step entails contacting people and persuading them to approve your ideas, the Minor Steps might be:

a) Identifying the people to contact
b) Putting your ideas on paper
c) Writing the letters or making the phone calls to establish the contacts
d) Transmitting your ideas
e) Evaluating the responses you get
f) Visiting the people individually or in groups to win their approval

. . . and so on.

As we discussed, Minor Steps tend to be the actions required to accomplish a Major Step. Repeat the planning process for each of your Minor Steps. Because these Minor Steps are generally action steps, you can be much more specific. Use Experience 28 to help you break down you Minor Steps into simple tasks you can accomplish in a single day or, better yet, in a single hour.

Put these tasks in sensible order and, again, find a satisfying reward you can tie to each one. Sometimes, though, the task itself is not rewarding. For example, a plan I once established for myself involved stuffing five hundred envelopes, addressing them, and mailing them. Another time, I had to hand staple two thousand magazines of forty-eight pages each! Neither of these tasks was a lot of fun, but they were essential to accomplishing my Major Step and my goal. You motivate yourself to accomplish such Minor Steps by creating rewards for them out of your imagination. For example, when I finished with the five hundred envelopes, I took off for the rest of the day and went for a long drive in the country. When I finished stapling the magazines, I treated myself to a meal in a fancy restaurant, where I ordered the best food and wine on the menu. Your tastes for pleasure may be different from mine, but they are undoubtedly just as strong. Create links between finishing the Minor Steps and giving yourself a reward and you will start making much faster progress toward your dream goal.

Experience 28

Converting Minor Steps to Simple Tasks

Instructions: In your personal notebook, break down each of your

Minor Steps into simple tasks you can do in a day or, better yet, in an hour. Use a separate page for each Minor Step.

1) At the top of the page, write the Minor Step toward which you are working, as well as the Major Step and the dream goal toward which it contributes.
2) Set a deadline for achieving the Minor Step.
3) List the simple tasks you can take to achieve the Minor Step you're planning. Try to break down the Step into small enough pieces so you can finish each task in a single day or, better yet, a single hour.
4) Put the simple tasks above into sensible order. Make two lists: one for tasks you must do in order, and a second one for tasks you can try to do anytime.
5) Number the simple tasks you've listed, and for each number, specify a reward you will receive (or give yourself) from each effort.

PUT EVERYTHING ON YOUR SCHEDULE

Look how far you've come from idle dreaming about your goal! You have a goal firmly in mind, fully described in detail, and you have it broken down into Major Steps, Minor Steps, and single tasks you can do in one sitting. Suddenly, the goal is a great deal closer than it was when it was little more than a dream. But you're not there yet. To make this dream goal a reality, you must use every possible technique for increasing your effectiveness and shaping your results to get what you want. And that includes scheduling.

Get out your calendar and begin scheduling each task in your overall plan. But don't discourage yourself by scheduling them all in a row for the next three weeks. Since your dream goal is probably fairly large, and since you have other responsibilities and other goals to pursue, schedule just one of these goal-oriented tasks a day, or one every other day, as far in advance as you possibly can. Then without fail, do what you have scheduled. The object is not to get there as fast as possible but, rather, to sustain your effort and get there for sure. Keep in mind that "Slow but steady wins the race."

As you complete a task, be sure to take and enjoy the reward you have linked to completing it. Like millions of others, you may have trouble being nice to yourself or giving yourself a reward. Do it anyway! These rewards serve a very real and important motivational purpose. Motivating yourself is an important skill, because it is an essential ingredient in any long-term effort to reach a goal.

MARK YOUR PROGRESS

Cross off each of the Steps as you complete it. And use a flowchart or a graph of some sort to keep your progress along the plan in full view as much as possible.

The graph of your progress is another reward that hits you where it helps whenever you see it. Don't hide the chart away or keep it a secret. You may be mistaking modesty for a self-defeating attitude that robs you of the fruits of victory even as you reach out to touch them. If you are working toward a dream goal you really want, and if you are making good progress, you deserve to feel good about your work and to share your good feelings with others.

SHARE YOUR METHODS
WITH OTHER PEOPLE

Like the progress chart, don't keep the Basic Achievement Program for Everyone Who Has a Mission or a Dream to yourself. Share your success, and your successful methods, with the people around you. Unlike you might in competitive situations, you suffer no penalty if other people achieve their goals or dreams. You lose nothing by sharing what you know. In fact, if you progress to where you can cooperate with others to achieve even larger dream goals or missions, sharing your methods may prove to be a Major Step toward the biggest and best goals you can conceive.

THE TIME LOG

The Time Log is the most accurate method of measuring how much time you spend on various activities throughout your work day, week, month, and year. At its simplest, the Time Log is a paper record you keep as you work. More elaborate systems entail a series of timers—each devoted to a specific category of activity—or a computerized timing system that more or less automatically tracks when you begin and when you end each activity.

As a general rule, people remember how they wish they had spent their time, not how they actually spent it. The Time Log puts an end to this convenient rewriting of history. By noting how you have spent each time interval throughout the day, your Time Log provides an incontrovertible document that details your actual time-use patterns.

INSTRUCTIONS FOR KEEPING YOUR TIME LOG

a) Draw up a list of your activities and projects. This preliminary list need not be exhaustive or detailed. A sample list might include any or all of the following:

General Items	Specific Items
Reading	Reading assignments by name or category.
Writing	Writing assignments by name or category.
Meetings	Meetings listed by specific purpose, location, or other category.
Travel	Commuting, business travel, local travel, deliveries and Pickups.
Free time	Work breaks, lunch breaks, study breaks, rest periods, waiting time, telephone time on hold.
Thinking	Thinking time, broken down into the time spent thinking about projects, responsibilities, or purposes. Consider the time you spend thinking about the future, the past, the present; about practical and impractical ideas; and about professional and personal goals.
Planning	Same category possibilities as thinking.
Telephone	Phone calls of specific types or to specific parties or locations.
Interruptions	Interruptions categorized according to: specific sources, specific purposes, specific people who interrupt you.

b) Augment your initial list by recording a clear, brief description of your activities for the first several entries in your Time Log. On subsequent entries, change or adapt your descriptions as necessary. After a few days or a week, you'll probably have a more complete and accurate list of your activities than you could have developed any other way.

c) Consolidate your categories into eight or fewer descriptions that thoroughly cover your major and minor projects. Eight is a good number of categories because it allows you to easily remember what each one is, yet it provides a good measure of diversity and can cover a very broad range of activities. If eight are not enough, you may want to create one set of eight categories for "work," another eight for "personal" time. Enter these categories by code number or abbreviation in column headings across the top of a form (see p. 266).

TIME LOG

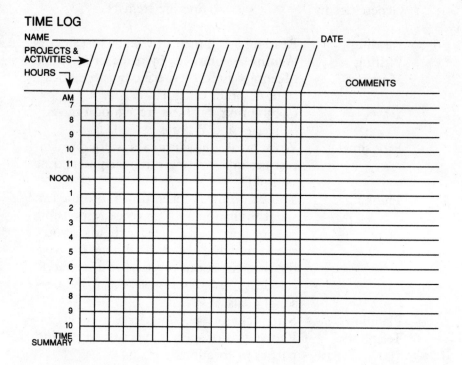

NAME _____ DATE _____

PROJECTS & ACTIVITIES→

HOURS

COMMENTS

AM
7
8
9
10
11
NOON
1
2
3
4
5
6
7
8
9
10
TIME
SUMMARY

d) Make enough copies of the Time Log form so you can have a fresh one every day, for as many days as it will take to convince you of its value. Several weeks' worth will probably be enough for a first printing.

e) Make an entry in your Time Log by simply putting a dot, a small "x," or any other fast and easy symbol on the chart. Place your mark at the appropriate intersection:

• *Horizontally* opposite the exact time you are marking the Time Log. For example, at 11:15 A.M. you would make your mark slightly below the line labeled "11."

• *Vertically* under the column heading that best describes what you are busy with at the time.

f) Fill in your Time Log as you go through your day. Don't plan on going back later to fix it up. Your memory will play tricks on you and record more about what you *think* you did than what you actually worked on. The best way to use the Time Log is to:

1) Make one entry at a time, only at regular intervals.
2) Record your main action of the past interval.
3) Choose your intervals so they best reflect your activities throughout the day.

g) Use fifteen-minute intervals, which are short enough for most people. But if you are in an especially fast-moving situation, you may want to use ten-minute or even shorter intervals. The picture you draw of your behavior patterns becomes more accurate with shorter intervals. However, shorter intervals double or triple the (very few) minutes your Time Log entries require. Choosing the interval is like deciding how to sample a truckload of apples. Do you take one, two, or three apples from each bushel basket? Do you sample from every basket, or every fourth? Or perhaps you taste only one apple from the whole truckload? Personal experience is crucial in making this choice. Here's a method to help you arrive at the best Time Log intervals for you:

1) Start by making entries every fifteen minutes.
2) After a full day of logging, shorten the interval for the next day to ten minutes if you find each entry requires a conscious choice of what to record and what to leave out.
3) Keep shortening the next day's interval by 25 to 35 percent until you find you usually have only one activity to record. This is an appropriate Time Log interval for you and your situation.

h) Note details of your activities right on the Time Log form to facilitate your later recall of what you did. These notes aid in your analysis and also boost the credibility of your Time Log results.
i) Evaluate your Time Log every few days to make any adjust-

ments you feel may be necessary in your procedure, your recording interval, or your headings. You may want to put
your ·categories in order, although after a few days you will
memorize their locations no matter how you arrange them.

j) After you are convinced your Time Logs are giving you an
accurate picture of your daily patterns, begin your analysis.

ANALYZING YOUR TIME-USE PATTERNS

a) Analyze by category. Add up all the time in each category on
your Time Log. Which projects take the most? Which projects the least? Does this reflect a fair evaluation of what the
results of these projects might be worth to you and/or your
future? Does this account for the entire period you thought
you logged? What happened to any unaccounted-for time?

b) Analyze by results. Compare the time in each category with
the results you achieve in that category. Are you getting a
fair measure of results per unit of time? Which categories
give you the most results per unit? Which categories the
least? Are you satisfied with this distribution?

c) Analyze by value. Which activities on your Time Log could
you eliminate from your schedule? Which ones deserve a
reduced effort? What would be the results, both positive and
negative, of eliminating certain items, or of reducing your
effort by 10 percent, 20 percent, or more? Which activities
on your Time Log deserve more attention? What results can
you expect from a 10 percent, 20 percent, or greater increase
in your allotment to such an activity?

d) Analyze by goal. Which of your goals are not well enough
represented by specific actions on your Time Log? Why don't
you appear to be working long enough to reach these goals?
If you are sure you want to reach these goals, what actions
will you add to your schedule to make better progress toward
them? What actions will you remove from your present
schedule to make room for these new activities?

e) Repeat as needed. When you finish the first few weeks of
Time Logging, you will have information to help you adjust
your efforts and achieve more of what you want. But after a

few months, you may well profit from keeping another Time Log. In fact, you can probably gain useful information and motivation from keeping Time Logs occasionally during the next several years. The new Logs will reveal improvements you have made, as well as others you still can make. As you gain experience with this tool, you may be able to reduce the number of weeks you must Log in a row to obtain accurate information.

A SCHEDULING
WORKSHEET

Sometimes a simple form can help you organize your whole day. The following sample scheduling worksheet—"To Do Today"—is set up and carefully ruled on the page to be useful, as well as to make copying easier. However, before you make too many copies, I advise you to test the form by using it for a few days or a week. Make any changes you want in the placement of the various sections or in their relative sizes. You may even want to add or delete one or two categories. Once you've settled on a form that works well for you, make copies freely and use a fresh one for each day.

INSTRUCTIONS FOR USING
THE SCHEDULING FORM

a) Tasks. List all the items you would like to accomplish during the day. Limit the number of items you schedule to what you honestly feel you can complete in a day. Too many items on your schedule only frustrate you. On the other hand, a completed schedule sheet at the end of the day invigorates you. Then: 1) cross of each item as you complete it, 2) select your next most important task and tackle it, and 3) add new items to the sheet as they come up, tackling each one when it becomes the "best" action available according to your Basic Choice.

You can fill in these worksheets in advance, thereby scheduling an entire week or a month in day-by-day detail. You can also use one form for the next calendar month (as in the Daily Prompter file), and at the beginning of the month distribute the items you collect on this form onto new copies of the form for each day's activities. Save the completed worksheets for a permanent record of your past performance. Look back from time to time to spot patterns and notice improvements.

b) Priority. You can simply list each task you want to accomplish. But the worksheet provides room for a more sophisticated list. The priority column gives you a place to rank all the items on your list by numerical order of importance, or high-, medium-, and low-priority groupings. The addition of a priority rating for each task helps you make a better Basic Choice of what to work on next. The following table provides a sample grading scale.

PRIORITY-GRADING SCALE

Point Grade	Definition
1	Handle immediately—emergency
2	Next item to work on
3	High priority—handle today
4	High priority—finish within one week
5	Medium priority—delegate for completion by deadline
6	Medium priority—fit into schedule and handle by deadline

NAME: _____

DATE: _____

TO DO TODAY

PRIORITY	TASKS	DEADLINE	ESTIMATED TIME	RESULTS & ACTUAL TIME USED	PHONE CALLS (name, purpose)

LETTERS/REPORTS TO WRITE	LONG RANGE (task, when due)

PEOPLE TO SEE/DISCUSSION TOPICS

7	Low priority—save for free time or slow-work season
8*	Of little value—ignore or throw out

---

*Note: This is a 7-point priority-rating scale. Items that have little or no priority fall off the scale into grade 8 for appropriate inaction.

c) Deadline. This column gives you a chance to note any applicable deadlines for each task. If a task has none, on your own initiative you may want to set one. Deadlines are another aid to better Basic Choices.

d) Estimated Time. The "Estimated Time" column serves two important purposes. First, it gives you a chance to indicate approximately how long you expect a task will take. With this information, you can select one that fits the time available to you. Second, you can later compare the "Estimated Time" with the "Actual Time Used" (in the next column) to improve your future estimates and thus learn to schedule more accurately.

e) Results and Actual Time Used. Filling in the "Results" column converts a used-up scheduling worksheet to a permanent record of your daily effectiveness. Your on-the-spot evaluations of the results you obtain from each effort: 1) form one important basis for judging how well you are making your Basic Choices, 2) help you pinpoint patterns of well-directed or wasted energy, and 3) promote the feeling of satisfaction you earn with your effort and thus provide motivation for you to do as well, or better, in the future.

f) Phone Calls. With the calls you want to make later in the day carefully noted, you can: 1) concentrate all your phone calls, and 2) consolidate several short topics of conversation with one person into a single, useful call. Whenever you reach for the telephone, reach instead for a pencil and jot the name, number, and reason for making that call. During the day, add to the same list any calls you must return. Then make all your calls during one or two "telephone periods" you establish in your day.

g) Letters/Reports to Write. Avoid writing individual letters, reports, notes, memos, or whatever—unless you can do them by hand in less than a minute. List the writing you must do in the appropriate section of the form, and do it all at once during special concentrated "writing periods" you designate.

h) People to See/Discussion Topics. The large white area at the bottom of the work sheet is your place to note both the people you want to talk to during the day and the items you want to discuss with each one. This helps you avoid running down the hall or around the town repeatedly. Instead, you make notes, then do all your visiting and talking in a concentrated session you fit into your schedule. You can even save up these items from one day to another and do all your visiting one afternoon a week!

i) Long range. This section is the place to jot notes on projects you want to start or work on in the future. As you're working, simply make a brief note on your scheduling worksheet to record any thoughts regarding a different project, then continue right on working. The thought is safely stored for action or consideration in the future.

At the end of each day, transfer items you have not completed to the next day's form. Try not to transfer an item more than once. Otherwise, your sheet will contain more baggage than action items.

Items you continually defer deserve reevaluation: 1) schedule them for when you will *really* be ready to act on them, 2) rework or reorganize them into something you can do now, or 3) discard them from your daily scheduling forms.

A GOAL-PLANNING
WORKBOOK

This Appendix contains the most useful goal-planning and goal-awareness experiences currently available, and integrates them into a short but comprehensive personal "Goal-Planning Workbook." You can use this section two different ways:

a) You can work through it while you read the book to help clarify your thinking, feeling, and dreaming, and to more readily integrate the techniques, attitudes, and ideas in the book with your special needs and aspirations.

b) You can come back to this Appendix anytime after you finish the book, and work through it as a short refresher on the basic goal-oriented ideas. When you do, you will also have the extra benefits of a renewed analysis of your desired goals and an updated look at the best means of achieving them.

Give the answers to each Experience in your personal notebook. This can be a permanent or a loose-leaf binder of any convenient size. Keep it with you, and write down all your personal notes, lists, and evaluations of your productivity and effectiveness. Over the next few months and years, you'll make this personal notebook into a valuable tool for self-improvement.

Experience C1

Defining Your Mission

Instructions: In your personal notebook, answer the following questions to the best of your ability.

1) For what accomplishments would you like to be known after your death?
2) Who are the people whose respect for your accomplishments (past and future) means the most to you? What accomplishments would they most appreciate from you?
3) Imagine yourself ten, twenty, thirty years from now. You will be relaxing and evaluating what you have accomplished in your life. Which of your achievements will make you the happiest? Which ones will you regret having pursued?
4) Think about where you were, what you were doing five, ten, fifteen years ago. Compare those days with your present situation. Have you made progress? In what direction(s)? Do you want to continue on? Might you receive more satisfaction, pleasure, or personal reward from some other direction(s)? Which one(s)?

Experience C2

Complete List of Desirable Goals

Instructions: This is a self-evaluation experience. Only your own feelings, beliefs, ideas, and judgments are relevant to how you will work through it.

1) In your personal notebook, list all the things you would like to do during your lifetime.

Samples:

PEOPLE TO SEE	PLACES TO GO	THINGS TO DO
Paul McCartney	Paris	Play in an All-Star Game

| Francis Ford Coppola | The moon | Star in a film |
| Stash Karczewski | Suriname | Earn $1,000,000 |

2) Count them. How many lifetimes would you need to do them all?

Experience C3

Self-Evaluation: Your Life and Career Goals

Instructions: This is a self-evaluation experience. Only your own feelings, beliefs, ideas, and judgments are relevant to how you will work through it.

1) In your personal notebook, make a list of ten "goals" you would like to achieve in your *personal life* during the next ten years. Each goal should describe an achievement—or an honor or reward recognizing an achievement—you would be proud to accomplish. Try to express each goal in specifics so you or anyone else can determine whether or not you achieve it. Examples: a) establish five close friendships with people you don't already know, b) travel around the world, c) go camping in Brazil, d) learn to play five songs on the guitar. List the present activities you might have to give up to have a chance to reach each of your personal goals.

2) In your personal notebook, make a list of ten "goals" you would like to achieve in your *career* during the next ten years. Each goal should describe an achievement—or an honor or reward recognizing an achievement—you would be proud to accomplish. Each goal should be expressed in specifics so you or anyone else can determine whether or not you achieve it. Examples: a) win an Academy Award, b) earn a promotion or a salary increase to a specific level, c) accomplish a specific project or specific amount of work by a certain deadline. List the present activities you might have to give up to have a chance to reach each of your career goals.

3) In your personal notebook, list two other activities, accomplishments, rewards, or recognitions that would bring you the highest level of satisfaction. List the present activities you might have to give up to have a chance to make these ideas a reality.

4) For each item you have listed, describe what further preparation you might undertake to help you along the way.

Experience C4

Self-Evaluation: Five Deadlines to Meet

Instructions: The object here is simply to establish for yourself at least five key deadlines for five projects that are important to you. The sooner you set some deadlines and make the personal determination to beat them, the sooner you can get the power of the deadline principle working for you.

1) In your personal notebook, list at least five important projects or activities you have been wanting to accomplish for a month or longer but have found no time to work on.

2) For each one, list the major steps you must complete to achieve your goal.

3) Estimate from your own experience (or just guess) how many days must elapse between starting and finishing each step. Add up all the days for each project or activity.

4) Use the total elapsed time you estimate you need for each activity to calculate a reasonable deadline for you to complete it. Take into account the order in which you want to tackle the five projects or activities, as well as your ability to work on several simultaneously. Write down your deadline next to each project on your list.

Experience C5

Self-Evaluation: Comparing Priorities and Activities

Instructions: This Experience helps you compare the projects and activities to which you *say* you give a high priority with the projects and activities to which you *actually* give your time.

1)   In your personal notebook, list the ten projects, activities, or goals you feel are your "highest priorities" for today and/or the next few weeks. If you like, use some of the same goals you listed in Experience C3.
2)   In your personal notebook, list the ten most demanding and/or most time-consuming projects, activities, or goals to which you gave time today.
3)   Compare your two lists: How many of your important goals received no attention from you today? How many "no priority" items—goals that never made it onto your "top ten" list—received a good portion of your effort?

Experience C6

Self-Evaluation: Goals You Can Work Toward Today

Instructions: In your personal notebook, list an important Life or Career goal from Experience C3.

1)   Establish a reasonable deadline for achieving this goal.
2)   Divide the goal into at least five smaller goals—smaller steps or achievements you must accomplish on the road to achieving the main goal itself. For each of these five smaller goals, establish a reasonable deadline.
3)   Further divide each smaller goal into several interim goals you must accomplish on the road to finishing this smaller goal. Establish a reasonable deadline for each interim goal.
4)   Finally, break down each of these interim goals into one or more one-day tasks that lead you toward completion of this interim step. These one-day steps represent the building blocks with which you can construct a "body of work" to represent you. Put these together in any reasonable order and you're bound to accomplish a great deal.

And not just any "great deal," but a specific type and style of accomplishment that spring from your own inner desires and reflect your unique interests, talents, and gifts. Almost certainly, no one else in the world could conceive of the projects you set for yourself, nor could they organize them in your special way. The same holds true of goals others set for you, but which you organize and divide into one-day tasks. Try to interest other people in doing some of the one-day tasks you've just outlined and you'll see how unique is your contribution.

Experience C7

Self-Evaluation: Choosing Tomorrow's Achievements

Instructions: Take a few moments and think about tomorrow. What have you planned? What are you going to work toward and accomplish?

1) In your personal notebook, list the projects, tasks, hobbies, or "general agenda" items you expect to pursue tomorrow. How many items can you list? Rank the items in two sets: first, the items you consider to be of "major" importance; and separately, the items you consider to be of "minor" importance.

2) For each "major" item, list at least one other project, task, hobby, or "general agenda" item you could pursue in its place. Try to emphasize items that better represent your stated goals and objectives.

3) For each "minor" item, list at least one other project, task, hobby, or "general agenda" item you could pursue in its place.

4) Go through these lists and select the items you will actually pursue tomorrow. Make sure you select only as many as you can reasonably handle. Beside each item you will pursue tomorrow, briefly note why you decided to pursue it at this time.

Experience C8

Self-Evaluation: Making the Basic Choice

Instructions: Use this Experience to help you choose between alternatives that seem to have equal claims upon your attention and effort. On closer inspection, you will probably find that one alternative has a stronger claim, based on what you want to accomplish and how you plan to proceed. Use these questions to start probing for that one most important opportunity to improve your results.

1) In your personal notebook, write down everything you might reasonably select as your next activity at work or at home.

2) For each option, list the potential results you might achieve, and the probability you will achieve them.

3) For each option, rank from 1 (least) to 5 (most) how directly it leads you toward one of your major goals.

4) For each option, rank its degree of urgency from 1 (least) to 5 (most). Also note the likely results if you do not pursue it at this time.

5) Which option seems to offer the most rewards or potential rewards right now?

INDEX

ABOUT THE AUTHOR

Robert Moskowitz is president of Crown Communications Group, a Los Angeles–based full-service consulting organization specializing in strategic management, white collar productivity, and office automation. He is the developer of the Personal Productivity Audit, an automated time-management instrument used by large organizations to provide individualized written reports on productivity-improvement strategies and techniques. Active as a professional writer since 1968, he has authored dozens of articles on diverse topics in national magazines.

Since 1972, he has written, directed, and produced more than a dozen top-selling audiocassette tape programs for major publishers. He has also written, directed, and produced industrial films and videos, including *Time Management for Supervisors,* which won the Silver Medal at the New York Film and Video Festival in 1979. His firm does writing, production, and distribution of consumer-information products, as well as advertising and public relations.

Mr. Moskowitz holds a bachelor's degree from the University of Pennsylvania. He is active in many local, national, and international communications organizations, including PEN, the Authors Guild, and Independent Writers of Southern California.